An Analysis of

Tony Judt's

Postwar
A History of Europe since 1945

Simon Young

Published by Macat International Ltd
24:13 Coda Centre, 189 Munster Road, London SW6 6AW.

Distributed exclusively by Routledge
2 Park Square, Milton Park, Abingdon, Oxon OX14 4RN
711 Third Avenue, New York, NY 10017, USA

Routledge is an imprint of the Taylor & Francis Group, an informa business

www.macat.com
info@macat.com

Cataloguing in Publication Data
A catalogue record for this book is available from the British Library.
Library of Congress Cataloguing-in-Publication Data is available upon request.
Cover illustration: Etienne Gilfillan

ISBN 978-1-912302-66-6 (hardback)
ISBN 978-1-912128-01-3 (paperback)
ISBN 978-1-912281-54-1 (e-book)

Notice
The information in this book is designed to orientate readers of the work under analysis,
to elucidate and contextualise its key ideas and themes, and to aid in the development
of critical thinking skills. It is not meant to be used, nor should it be used, as a
substitute for original thinking or in place of original writing or research. References and
notes are provided for informational purposes and their presence does not constitute
endorsement of the information or opinions therein. This book is presented solely for
educational purposes. It is sold on the understanding that the publisher is not engaged
to provide any scholarly advice. The publisher has made every effort to ensure that
this book is accurate and up-to-date, but makes no warranties or representations with
regard to the completeness or reliability of the information it contains. The information
and the opinions provided herein are not guaranteed or warranted to produce particular
results and may not be suitable for students of every ability. The publisher shall not be
liable for any loss, damage or disruption arising from any errors or omissions, or from
the use of this book, including, but not limited to, special, incidental, consequential or
other damages caused, or alleged to have been caused, directly or indirectly, by the
information contained within.

CONTENTS

THE MACAT LIBRARY

The Macat Library is a series of unique academic explorations of seminal works in the humanities and social sciences – books and papers that have had a significant and widely recognised impact on their disciplines. It has been created to serve as much more than just a summary of what lies between the covers of a great book. It illuminates and explores the influences on, ideas of, and impact of that book. Our goal is to offer a learning resource that encourages critical thinking and fosters a better, deeper understanding of important ideas.

Each publication is divided into three Sections: Influences, Ideas, and Impact. Each Section has four Modules. These explore every important facet of the work, and the responses to it.

This Section-Module structure makes a Macat Library book easy to use, but it has another important feature. Because each Macat book is written to the same format, it is possible (and encouraged!) to cross-reference multiple Macat books along the same lines of inquiry or research. This allows the reader to open up interesting interdisciplinary pathways.

To further aid your reading, lists of glossary terms and people mentioned are included at the end of this book (these are indicated by an asterisk [*] throughout) – as well as a list of works cited.

Macat has worked with the University of Cambridge to identify the elements of critical thinking and understand the ways in which six different skills combine to enable effective thinking.
Three allow us to fully understand a problem; three more give us the tools to solve it. Together, these six skills make up the **PACIER** model of critical thinking. They are:

ANALYSIS – understanding how an argument is built
EVALUATION – exploring the strengths and weaknesses of an argument
INTERPRETATION – understanding issues of meaning

CREATIVE THINKING – coming up with new ideas and fresh connections
PROBLEM-SOLVING – producing strong solutions
REASONING – creating strong arguments

To find out more, visit **WWW.MACAT.COM.**

CRITICAL THINKING AND *POSTWAR*

Primary critical thinking skill: REASONING
Secondary critical thinking skill: CREATIVE THINKING

Tony Judt decided to write *Postwar* in 1989, the year the collapse of the Soviet Union provided European history with a rare example of a clearly-signposted 'end of an era'.

It's scarcely surprising, then, that the great virtue of Judt's book is the clarity and the breadth of its account of postwar Europe. His book coalesces around one central theme: the idea that the whole of the history of this period can be explained as an unravelling of the consequences of World War II. A bold claim, but Judt's exceptional ability to create strong, well-structured, inclusive arguments to allows him to pull it off convincingly.

Judt's work is also a fine example of creative thinking, in that he excels in connecting things together in new and interesting ways. This virtue extends from his unusual ability to combine the best elements of the Anglo-American and the French historiographical traditions – the latter informing his strong interest in the importance of cultural history – to his unwillingness to allow himself to be constrained by historical category and ultimately to his linguistic abilities. *Postwar* is, above all, a triumph of integration, something that is only made possible by its author's flair for creating strong, persuasive arguments.

ABOUT THE AUTHOR OF THE ORIGINAL WORK

Tony Judt was born in London in 1948, but spent most of his career in America. He studied history at Cambridge and then earned his doctorate in France. His first major writings were about France's historical left-wing movements, particularly the French Socialist Party. Judt started working on *Postwar: A History of Europe since 1945* in 1989 when he was employed by New York University. Published in 2005, it went on to win numerous honors; in 2006 it was shortlisted for the nonfiction Pulitzer Prize and captured the Arthur Ross Book Award. Judt built a storied career as a public intellectual on the back of this success, and died in 2010 after a very public battle with the degenerative and fatal neurological disease, amyotrophic lateral sclerosis.

ABOUT THE AUTHOR OF THE ANALYSIS

Dr Simon Young holds a PhD in history from Cambridge and now teaches at the Italica Academy in Florence. His research focuses chiefly on the traditions of English and Irish popular literature.

ABOUT MACAT

GREAT WORKS FOR CRITICAL THINKING

Macat is focused on making the ideas of the world's great thinkers accessible and comprehensible to everybody, everywhere, in ways that promote the development of enhanced critical thinking skills.

It works with leading academics from the world's top universities to produce new analyses that focus on the ideas and the impact of the most influential works ever written across a wide variety of academic disciplines. Each of the works that sit at the heart of its growing library is an enduring example of great thinking. But by setting them in context – and looking at the influences that shaped their authors, as well as the responses they provoked – Macat encourages readers to look at these classics and game-changers with fresh eyes. Readers learn to think, engage and challenge their ideas, rather than simply accepting them.

'Macat offers an amazing first-of-its-kind tool for interdisciplinary learning and research. Its focus on works that transformed their disciplines and its rigorous approach, drawing on the world's leading experts and educational institutions, opens up a world-class education to anyone.'

Andreas Schleicher
Director for Education and Skills, Organisation for Economic Co-operation and Development

'Macat is taking on some of the major challenges in university education … They have drawn together a strong team of active academics who are producing teaching materials that are novel in the breadth of their approach.'

Prof Lord Broers,
former Vice-Chancellor of the University of Cambridge

'The Macat vision is exceptionally exciting. It focuses upon new modes of learning which analyse and explain seminal texts which have profoundly influenced world thinking and so social and economic development. It promotes the kind of critical thinking which is essential for any society and economy. This is the learning of the future.'

Rt Hon Charles Clarke, former UK Secretary of State for Education

'The Macat analyses provide immediate access to the critical conversation surrounding the books that have shaped their respective discipline, which will make them an invaluable resource to all of those, students and teachers, working in the field.'

Professor William Tronzo, University of California at San Diego

WAYS IN TO THE TEXT

KEY POINTS

- Tony Judt (1948–2010), author of *Postwar: A History of Europe since 1945*, was a British historian based for most of his professional life in the United States.

- Published in 2005, *Postwar* offered the first detailed history of Europe between the end of World War II* in 1945 and the collapse of European communism* between 1989 and 1991.

- In *Postwar*, Tony Judt argued that the period (1945–91) was significantly marked by the consequences and the memory of World War II.

Who Was Tony Judt?

The author of *Postwar: A History of Europe since 1945* (2005), Tony Judt, was born in London in 1948 to a poor Jewish immigrant family.[1] He studied history at King's College, Cambridge and carried out his doctorate work in France.[2] Judt specialized in political and intellectual history; five of his first six books were about modern and contemporary France.[3]

Judt taught in Britain and, for the most part, in the United States. By his forties, he had a growing interest in Eastern Europe, learning to speak Czech in the 1980s and occasionally travelling to communist Czechoslovakia where he associated with dissidents (people whose political opinions brought them into conflict with the state).[4] In 1995 he founded the Erich Maria Remarque Institute* in New York, an organization dedicated to the study of contemporary Europe, which he headed. In these years his prestige in Britain and the United States grew as he published in various national and international periodicals.[5]

Judt decided to write *Postwar* in December 1989. The collapse of Soviet* domination in Eastern Europe was then well underway (the Soviet Union was a federation of communist states in Eastern Europe, dominated by Russia). An epoch of European history was ending; Judt wanted to record the events that would define the period. It took him until 2005 to publish his book; during this time he ran a busy institute, married, had two children, and survived cancer.[6]

Judt died in 2010, five years after the book's publication. He had suffered for two years from amyotrophic lateral sclerosis,* a degenerative and fatal neurological disease.[7]

What Does *Postwar* Say?

According to *Postwar*, World War II lasted for 50 years in Europe—decades longer than the fighting of 1939–45; the peace involved thrashing out the many issues that had emerged in the years of conflict.[8] The year 1989 and the collapse of Soviet communism in Eastern Europe marked the end of this process and the last of the problems produced by the war.[9] Judt's epilogue, "From the House of the Dead," returns to the war and its memory; in it, he concludes that shared expressions of regret for the Holocaust*—the industrial murder of millions of people, largely Jewish, at the hands of the extreme right-wing Nazi* regime of Germany—had become the mark of membership in the true European community.[10]

Judt also offers a new definition of Europe. Most historians of the Cold War*—a period of political tension between the United States and the Soviet Union that lasted from 1948 to 1991—accepted a division between democratic Western Europe and the communist East and had tended to concentrate on large countries such as Germany and France. Judt objected, arguing that the East–West division prevented scholars from understanding postwar Europe, contending instead that it was necessary to take the history of Western and Eastern Europe together.[11]

Further, Judt looked beyond the large European countries, considering also small and medium-sized ones. *Postwar* has, of course, references to the large nations, such as its consideration of the privatizations in Britain in the 1980s, in the course of which, state-owned energy and communications institutions were sold to private business.[12] But some passages also relate to smaller countries. Judt writes, for example, on Czechoslovak intellectuals and on Scandinavian eugenics*—a pseudoscience dedicated to improving human genetics through selective breeding and sterilization.[13]

Postwar proved an instant classic. No other book had given an overview of Cold War European history for both East and West in such depth. Almost universally praised in reviews in 2005 and 2006, *Postwar* was shortlisted for prestigious literary prizes such as the Pulitzer* and Samuel Johnson prizes and won the Arthur Ross Book Award. In the first decade after its publication, *Postwar* sold thousands of paperback and audio copies and was translated into a dozen different European and Asian languages. Judt's success was not limited to the general public; *Postwar* quickly became a touchstone for scholars working on contemporary European history.

Why Does *Postwar* Matter?

Postwar represents a fine example of modern narrative history. Judt successfully transcends his background in political history* (the history of political ideas, political groups, and so on) to combine political, economic, social, and cultural history. Judt not only brought these different strands together but spliced them with sometimes disconcerting results: he compares for example, the Sex Pistols, an anarchic British punk* band, to the Red Army Faction,* a roughly contemporary German terrorist group.[14]

Judt's creation of a new historical space in *Postwar* marked his most important achievement. Few historians had covered the post-World War II period in Europe, or had only done so while writing histories of the Cold War or European integration*—the movement towards closer political and economic ties between the nations of Western Europe from 1949.[15] Judt's work changed this: though he mapped out a period that stretched from the war's end to the collapse of Soviet communism, insisting that east and west Europe, small and big countries, be studied together.[16] Until this point, written histories had considered the postwar period and World War II as a single subject, or examined more specific geographical areas.

The work's success can be measured by its influence. From the English-speaking world, Dan Stone* in *Goodbye to All That?* and Keith Lowe* in *Savage Continent*—two widely acclaimed recent works on contemporary European history—both pay tribute to the centrality of *Postwar* in creating a new historical territory.[17] Judt carved out a space for recent European history, which was no longer read solely in terms of American, Soviet, or Cold War concerns. Judt and his successors would, as a result, find it easier to cover European themes such as social democracy* (a social and economic system in which a state intervenes in its economy to alleviate poverty and to provide public services).[18]

Finally, Judt was fascinated by the subject of memory. Remembering and *refusing* to remember, he recognizes, proved key for Europe as it returned to peace after World War II. Some countries remembered selectively: the French and Italians concentrated on their resistance* movements to expunge the memory of humiliating defeats, for example.[19] Other countries chose to forget: Germany avoided discussions of the Shoah* (another term for the Holocaust) until the 1960s.[20] Judt's writings on communal memories are vital for postwar European history—but historians and political scientists working in other contexts have employed them as well.[21]

NOTES

1 Tony Judt with Timothy Snyder, *Thinking the Twentieth Century* (London: Penguin, 2012), 1–12.

2 Judt with Snyder, *Thinking the Twentieth Century*, 140–50.

3 Tony Judt, *La reconstruction du Parti Socialiste, 1920–26* (Paris: Fondation nationale des sciences politiques, 1976); Tony Judt, *Socialism in Provence, 1871–1914: A Study in the Origins of the Modern French Left* (Cambridge: Cambridge University Press, 1979); Tony Judt, *Marxism and the French Left: Studies on Labour and Politics in France, 1830–1981* (Oxford: Oxford University Press, 1986); Tony Judt, *Past Imperfect: French Intellectuals, 1944–1956* (Berkeley, CA: University of California Press, 1992); Tony Judt, *A Grand Illusion? An Essay on Europe* (New York: Hill and Wang, 1996); Tony Judt, *The Burden of Responsibility: Blum, Camus, Aron, and the French Twentieth Century* (Chicago, IL: University of Chicago Press, 1998).

4 Tony Judt, *The Memory Chalet* (London: William Heinemann, 2010), 171–2.

5 Tony Judt, *Reappraisals: Reflections on the Forgotten Twentieth Century* (London: William Heinemann, 2008).

6 Jennifer Homans, "Introduction: In Good Faith," in Tony Judt, *When The Facts Change: Essays 1995–2010* (London: William Heinemann, 2015), 2–3.

7 Judt, *The Memory Chalet*, 15–21.

8 Tony Judt, *Postwar: A History of Europe since 1945* (New York: Penguin, 2005), 10.

9 Judt, *Postwar*, 9–10.

10 Judt, *Postwar*, 803–31.

11 Judt, *Postwar*, 5–6.

12 Judt, *Postwar*, 541.

13 Judt, *Postwar*, 368, 566–8.

14 Judt, *Postwar*, 481–2.

15 Geoff Eley, "Europe after 1945," *History Workshop Journal* 65 (2008): 195–212.

16 Judt, *Postwar*, 5–6.

17 Dan Stone, *Goodbye to All That? The Story of Europe since 1945* (Oxford: Oxford University Press, 2014), IX, 42, 47, 143, 162, 165, 167, 186, 255–6, 263–4, 284, 291; *Keith Lowe, Savage Continent: Europe in the Aftermath of World War II* (London: Viking, 2012), XVII.

18 Judt, *Postwar*, 7–8.

19 Judt, *Postwar*, 33–4.

20 Judt, *Postwar*, 810–12.

21 See Peter Hayes, *How Was It Possible? A Holocaust Reader* (Lincoln, NE: University of Nebraska Press, 2015), 801–20.

SECTION 1
INFLUENCES

MODULE 1
THE AUTHOR AND THE
HISTORICAL CONTEXT

KEY POINTS

- *Postwar* is the only history of contemporary Europe to comprehensively cover all aspects of the history of East and West, small countries and large, in the decades following World War II.*

- Tony Judt lived through many of the events he described— and *Postwar* reflects his experience of the British welfare state* (a system affording economic assistance to vulnerable members of society) and European social democracy* more generally.

- Tony Judt was able to write about postwar Eastern Europe thanks to a decision taken to learn Czech in middle age, opening up the East to him.

Why Read This Text?

Postwar: A History of Europe since 1945 (2005) by Tony Judt offers an account of the recent European past. In it, Judt set out to write the story of the continent from Germany's surrender to the Allies* (the forces led by Great Britain, the Soviet Union, and the United States) in May 1945 to the collapse of the Soviet* bloc—the federation of states dominated by the Soviet Union—between 1989 and 1991. To write 50 years of history for an area as varied and as complex as Europe would, in itself, have amounted to a remarkable achievement. However, Judt deals with both the democratic West and the communist* East in a single volume—most commentators had dealt with one subject or the other—and gives the history of European nations of all degrees of

❝ In my own case, both in *Postwar* and in more recent
memoiristic writings, I have taken care to ground
my perspective in my time and place of birth—my
education, my family, class and generation. ❞

Tony Judt, *Thinking the Twentieth Century*

power, size, and influence. More, he avoids a simple political narrative
in favor of an approach in which culture, economics, military affairs,
and social history play a significant part.

Judt ties these threads together with a simple, strong argument: that
recent European history is the playing out of the consequences of
World War II. Thanks in large part to this unique approach, *Postwar*
became an instant classic.

Author's Life

Tony Judt was born in 1948 in Putney, a district of west London, to a
family of secular Jewish émigrés. His grandparents had escaped
persecution in eastern and central Europe to come to Britain, and
some members of his extended family had suffered under the Nazis.[*1]
Indeed, Judt was named after a cousin, Toni, who had been murdered
at the notorious Nazi concentration camp Auschwitz.[*2]

Judt went to a local grammar school* (a UK state school at which
places are given according to merit), going on to the University of
Cambridge, where he studied history.[3] He specialized in modern and
contemporary French politics and intellectual life, pursuing his
doctorate work in France.[4] He published first on France's historical
left-wing movements, particularly the French Socialist* Party. By his
twenties, he already had a reputation for writing a French style of
intellectual history little appreciated in Britain.[5] Ultimately his brand
of history writing proved better suited to American universities, where
he spent most of his adult career as a teacher, writer, and administrator.[6]

Judt conceived *Postwar* while employed by New York University in 1989. His knowledge of the Czech language, he later stated, unlocked for him the history of Eastern Europe.[7] In December 1989, he was ending a trip to the newly free Czechoslovakia and found himself in Vienna, Austria—the crossroads between Western and Eastern Europe. Hearing the news of the fall of communist Romania on the radio in his taxi, he recognized that a period of European history was coming to an end.[8] In this moment he decided to chronicle the continent's recent history in the East *and* West.

Postwar was written, for the most part, while he served as the director of the Erich Maria Remarque Institute* in New York, a body dedicated to scholarship of contemporary European history, which he founded in 1995. Judt died in 2010, five years after the publication of *Postwar*, following a battle with the degenerative neurological disease amyotrophic lateral sclerosis.*[9]

Author's Background

As a child of postwar Britain, Judt lived through much of the period he documented.[10] Coming from a poor district of London, he benefitted from the newly created British welfare state—a fact he references in *Postwar*.[11] He enjoyed, for example, good and free public education at secondary and university levels. As a result, Judt was a passionate supporter of social democracy and generous welfare provisions. This emerges particularly in one of his final works, *Ill Fares the Land*,[12] but Judt also gives social democracy a special place in *Postwar*, claiming it to be a characteristically European system.[13]

Judt's father was an enthusiastic socialist and so Judt grew up in a left-wing intellectual environment.[14] However, his father was also anti-Soviet and Judt followed his father in this ("Soviet" here refers to the Soviet Union, a federation of communist states in Eastern and Central Europe dominated by Russia). It is interesting, for example, that he studied the French Socialist Party as a young man but not the powerful Soviet-backed French Communist Party.[15] And so *Postwar*, unsurprisingly, casts a critical eye on the Soviet Union's occupation of Eastern Europe after 1945 and Soviet imperial might in general.

Judt's Jewish heritage also proved important to him. Never particularly religious, in his teens and early twenties he supported the Zionist* movement's desire to see a Jewish state established in the historical site of ancient Israel.[16] However, his sense of Jewishness gave him a complicated and compound identity—the main reason he seems never to have felt entirely British.[17] He also had a strong interest in some parts of middle Europe from where his Jewish relatives had come.[18] This part of Judt's identity emerges in *Postwar* through his interest in multicultural* societies, particularly the rich, varied communities once so common in central Europe before the juggernaut of war destroyed them.[19]

NOTES

1   Tony Judt with Timothy Snyder, *Thinking the Twentieth Century* (London: Penguin, 2012), 1–6.

2   Tony Judt, *The Memory Chalet* (London: William Heinemann, 2010), 210–16.

3   Judt, *The Memory Chalet*, 49–56, 135–46.

4   Judt with Snyder, *Thinking the Twentieth Century*, 140–7.

5   Judt with Snyder, *Thinking the Twentieth Century*, 149.

6   Judt, *The Memory Chalet*, 157–64.

7   Judt, *The Memory Chalet*, 171–2.

8   Tony Judt, *Postwar: A History of Europe since 1945* (New York: Penguin, 2005), 1.

9   Judt, *The Memory Chalet*, 15–21.

10 Judt with Snyder, *Thinking the Twentieth Century*, 395–6.

11 Judt, *Postwar*, 75.

12 Tony Judt, *Ill Fares the Land* (London: Allen Lane, 2010).

13 Judt, *Postwar*, 360–89.

14 Judt with Snyder, *Thinking the Twentieth Century*, 75–7.

15 Judt with Snyder, *Thinking the Twentieth Century*, 146.

16 Judt with Snyder, *Thinking the Twentieth Century*, 106–17.

17 Jennifer Homans, "Introduction: In Good Faith," in Tony Judt, *When The Facts Change: Essays 1995–2010* (London: William Heinemann, 2015), 2.

18 Judt with Snyder, *Thinking the Twentieth Century*, 1–4.

19 Judt, *Postwar*, 8–9.

MODULE 2
ACADEMIC CONTEXT

KEY POINTS

- Postwar British and French historians had favored social and economic matters over more traditional political and intellectual narrative history.

- Tony Judt had a life-long interest in new historical concerns such as social history (history that considers the experience and contribution of ordinary men and women).

- *Postwar* is influenced by the assumptions and methods of historical analysis that characterize left-wing approaches to the discipline.

The Work in its Context

Tony Judt's *Postwar: A History of Europe since 1945* is a work of history that reflects the aims and methods of the discipline as it is practiced in the two countries where Judt learnt his craft: Britain and France. British history writing is often said to be more concrete and interested in facts; French writing is often understood to be more interested in ideas.[1] Historians from both countries, however, have generally focused on narrative history—the telling of a story.

Traditional French history had been challenged, from the late 1920s, by the *Annales* School,* named after a French historical journal of the period. *Annales* historians favored a centuries-long view of how social and economic affairs evolved, and drew on the methods and interests of academic disciplines other than history; they were fascinated by the "long sweep of history" rather than the traditional political history of great men and women. In the 1960s, when Judt trained at Cambridge, history studies there were dominated by a

> ❝ Nobody can write the history of the twentieth
> century like that of any other era, if only because
> nobody can write about his or her lifetime as one can
> write about a period known only from outside, at
> second or third-hand, from sources of the period or the
> works of later historians. ❞
>
> Eric Hobsbawm, *Age of Extremes*

British approach derived from the *Annales* School.[2] This brand of
"new" social or "total" history* was more Marxist* than its French
cousin—that is, it was influenced by the analysis of social and
economic history associated with the political philosopher Karl
Marx.* In other respects, British social historians had similar aims:
they excavated changing social and cultural habits, often over long
periods of time.[3]

As a whole, *Postwar* represents an original hybrid of British and
French history and of the old and new history writing. The book
borrows from traditional political narrative history: in describing how
Soviet* control in Eastern Europe collapsed, for example, it shows
stylistic similarities to a traditional nineteenth-century narrative.[4] It
also includes, however, examples of the new history that blended
cultural, economic, and social details—so Judt's writing on postwar
affluence is modern in the way it interweaves statistics, facts, and
anecdotes from these three areas.[5] *Postwar's* concentration on the
history of ideas, meanwhile, is more French than British in style: in its
pages on "the great age of Theory," the 1960s, Judt implies that new
philosophies can shape and explain society.[6]

Overview of the Field

Few historians can write ambitious overviews of a continent's history
through half a century. Just three major works on Europe were

published while Judt researched and wrote *Postwar*, all from British historians: two of these were Norman Davies'* *Europe: A History* (1998), a book that Judt strongly criticized,[7] and Mark Mazower's* *Dark Continent* (2000), a book that Judt praised but did not treat as a model.[8] The Marxist historian Eric Hobsbawm* wrote the third,[9] publishing before his death four volumes describing world history (though with a strong concentration on Europe) from the late eighteenth to the late twentieth century. The final volume, *The Age of Extremes: The Short Twentieth Century, 1914–1991* (1994),[10] proved an inspiration for *Postwar*.

In *The Age of Extremes* Hobsbawm accomplished what Judt aspired to do in *Postwar*: a traditional history that combined social, cultural, economic, and political elements. And like Judt, Hobsbawm was not a typical "British historian," having been born in Egypt to a German-speaking family. Although he drew on the methods of the new "total history," an approach to writing history in which the master themes in the history of a period are sought for in the smallest specifics of social, religious, and cultural life, he criticized what he saw as its descent into useless social details.[11] Instead, Hobsbawm used an idiosyncratic and personal style, sometimes commenting, like Judt, on his own experiences in the history he chronicled.[12]

Academic Influences

Judt himself combined both French and British, traditional, and new influences that stemmed from his education as a historian.[13] He studied under and was inspired by John Dunn* and Quentin Skinner* at Cambridge—scholars who focused on the history of political thought with a view to better understanding the social context in which works had been written.[14] It is interesting, too, that by the early 1980s British historians viewed Judt as having "gone native" in France and as a result being too "French" in his historical approach to find ready employment in a British university.[15]

But if Judt was open to new and non–British currents, he also showed himself in some respects conservative in historical terms. In 1979, he wrote an article that attacked, in the most strident terms, the excesses of social history,[16] and he continued to attack "cultural studies"*—a recently founded discipline dedicated to the shifting meanings and habits of contemporary cultures—until his death.[17]

In *Postwar*, Judt consciously places himself in a tradition of historians who wrote ambitious histories about modern states and regions. In fact, he mentions in his preface four works of general European history "to which I have looked for inspiration and example":[18]

• Eric Hobsbawm's *The Age of Extremes* (actually a world history but concentrating on Europe)
• George Lichtheim's* *Europe in the Twentieth Century*
• A. J. P. Taylor's* *English History 1914–1945*
• François Furet's* *The Passing of an Illusion: The Idea of Communism in the Twentieth Century* (first published in French in 1995).[19]

These four books provide a useful guide to Judt's historical values. All are fundamentally written from the left, while two (Hobsbawm's and Lichtheim's) are from the Marxist left. Written as narratives, the four books also range in easy, ambitious fashion across historical categories that deal with society, economics, culture, and, above all, politics. Hobsbawm and Lichtheim were remarkable in that they dealt with Eastern and Western European history in very great detail. It was a divide few scholars had dared to attempt—and one Judt would leap over, writing a great work of contemporary history.

NOTES

1   Pim den Boer, "Historical Writing in France, 1800–1914," in *The Oxford History of Historical Writing: 1800–1945*, ed. Stuart Macintyre et al. (Oxford: Oxford University Press, 2011), 198–201.

2   Tony Judt with Timothy Snyder, *Thinking the Twentieth Century* (London: Penguin, 2012), 396.

3   David Feldman and John Lawrence, "Introduction: Structures and Transformations in British Historiography," in *Structures and Transformations in Modern British History*, ed. David Feldman and John Lawrence (Cambridge: Cambridge University Press, 2011), 1.

4   Tony Judt, *Postwar: A History of Europe since 1945* (New York: Penguin, 2005), 585–633.

5   Judt, *Postwar*, 337–53.

6   Judt, *Postwar*, 398–401.

7   Tony Judt, *When the Facts Change* (London: William Heinemann, 2015), 47–64.

8   Tony Judt, "Democracy as an Aberration," *New York Times*, February 7, 1999, accessed October 24, 2015, https://www.nytimes.com/books/99/02/07/reviews/990207.07judtlt.html.

9   Judt with Snyder, *Thinking the Twentieth Century*, 155.

10   Eric Hobsbawm, *The Age of Revolution: 1789–1848* (London: New English Library, 1965); *The Age of Capital, 1848–1875* (London: Weidenfeld & Nicolson, 1975); *The Age of Empire, 1875–1914* (London: Cardinal 1987); and *The Age of Extremes* (London: Michael Joseph, 1994).

11   Eric Hobsbawm, '"Social History to the History of Society,'," *Daedalus* 100 (1971), 20–45.

12   Hobsbawm, *Age of Extremes*, 4.

13   Judt with Snyder, *Thinking the Twentieth Century*, 140–8.

14   John Dunn, *The Political Thought of John Locke* (Cambridge: Cambridge University Press, 1969); Quentin Skinner, *Machiavelli* (Oxford: Oxford University Press, 1981).

15   Judt with Snyder, *Thinking the Twentieth Century*, 149.

16   Tony Judt, "A Clown in Regal Purple: Social History and the Historians," *History Workshop Journal* 7 (1979).

17   Judt with Snyder, *Thinking the Twentieth Century*, 154–5.

18   Judt, *Postwar*, xiv.

19   Eric Hobsbawm, *The Age of Extremes* (London: Michael Joseph, 1994); George Lichtheim, *Europe in the Twentieth Century* (London: Cardinal, 1974); A. J. P. Taylor, *English History 1914–1945* (Oxford: Oxford University Press, 1965); François Furet, *The Passing of an Illusion: The Idea of Communism in the Twentieth Century* (Chicago: University of Chicago Press, 1999).

MODULE 3
THE PROBLEM

KEY POINTS

- The writing of large-scale narrative history—such as that of the 50 years of the recent European past related in *Postwar*—has presented historians with certain difficulties.

- A handful of other scholars had attempted massive narrative histories of contemporary Europe: the British historian Eric Hobsbawm* and the German American historian George Lichtheim,* for example, wrote overviews from a Marxist* perspective.

- While Tony Judt followed Hobsbawm and Lichtheim's general model in writing *Postwar*, his work is not Marxist like theirs: *Postwar* also combines, to a greater extent than Lichtheim, social, political, cultural, and economic history.

Core Question

In *Postwar: A History of Europe since 1945,* Tony Judt turned to World War II* as the interpretative key to both Western and communist* Eastern Europe in the years 1945–91.[1] For him, the period is characterized and defined by the continent's effort to work out the consequences of the conflict of 1939 to 1945.

Judt recognized himself as something of a pioneer in writing this kind of ambitious East–West, 50-year history.[2] With the exception of limited histories of European integration*[3] (the move towards closer political and economic union between the states of Western Europe) and the Cold War*[4] (the long period of tension between the Soviet Union* and its allies, and the United States and its allies, that markedly influenced global politics following World War II), Europe's postwar

> ❝ Whatever its shortcomings [*Postwar*] is rare for
> the determination with which I set out to integrate
> Europe's two halves into a common story. In a
> way, *Postwar* echoes my own attempt to become an
> integrated historian of Europe rather than a disabused
> critic of French historical fashion. ❞
>
> Tony Judt, *The Memory Chalet*

years had been little studied until 1991. There were conspicuously few book-length works on the subject.

A striking contrast existed between the history of World War II—which had been exhaustively researched—and the neglected history of the 1950s. The period was perhaps just too recent or, it has been suggested, unresolved in some ways.[5] Meanwhile in Eastern Europe, totalitarian* governments (governments that greatly intervene in the lives of their citizens, at the cost of their liberty) made it difficult or even dangerous to study the immediate past in a scientific fashion.[6]

But the collapse of the Soviet bloc between 1989 and 1991 created a new reality in Europe. In the East, many previously communist states were absorbed into the European Union* (a political and economic union formed in 1993). Scholars gained greater access to Eastern European archives after the communist collapse;[7] this coincided with a boom in history writing in postcommunist countries, as local historians examined the events leading to, and the evolution of, communism itself. Judt benefitted from this new spirit in the East and was empowered to write *Postwar* to contrast Eastern and Western European experiences of the recent past. Before 2005, when *Postwar* was finally published, relatively few general narratives had seen the light of day. Even today *Postwar* is perhaps the only satisfactory history that embraces *all* of Cold War Europe.

The Participants

In crafting his particular style of narrative, Judt studied and was inspired by two important writers on the postwar period: the German American historian George Lichtheim, author of *Europe in the Twentieth Century*, and the British historian Eric Hobsbawm, who wrote *The Age of Extremes*. Lichtheim published *Europe* in 1972 and wrote his narrative history of the continent up until the 1960s, meaning he had fewer years than Hobsbawm or Judt to assess the continent's postwar evolution. Lichtheim's work, unusually covering both East and West, is written from a Marxist perspective—although, unlike Hobsbawm (but like Judt), Lichtheim remained consistently anti-Soviet.

Although Hobsbawm also takes a Marxist view in his 1994 book, he offers a narrative on a global scale that reflects some nostalgia for the Soviet Union; in fact, Hobsbawm remained unrepentantly pro-Soviet until his death.[8] Hobsbawm divides the postwar period into the "Golden Age" (a period of postwar economic boom) and the "Landslide" (a period, following the 1970s, in which economic stagnation and communism's collapse led to new uncertainties).[9] Credit for helping to create the postwar period as a defined territory in the discipline of history should go in equal measure to Hobsbawm and Judt. Hobsbawm was the first major historian to write a general account of the postwar period—and crucially, he chose World War II and the fall of the Soviet bloc as natural bookends for the period.

The Contemporary Debate

Tony Judt enjoyed good relations with both Lichtheim and Hobsbawm. While he never actually met Lichtheim, the German intellectual had written an important reference letter that won Judt his first academic job.[10] Judt admired Lichtheim's work to the degree that he dedicated a book to him.[11] Meanwhile, Judt wrote of happy meetings with Hobsbawm,[12] who himself authored one of the most penetrating reflections on Judt shortly after his death in 2010.[13] Judt also wrote that he had far more in common with Hobsbawm as a historian than with his younger contemporaries.[14]

But if Judt had a personal relationship with both writers, this did not mean that he agreed with them in all things. He was especially critical, for example, of Hobsbawm's pro-Soviet history writing.[15] And while he admired Lichtheim, Judt wrote *Postwar* using a full battery of social, economic, political, and cultural facts; Lichtheim was much more philosophical and favored European thought and politics in his *Europe in the Twentieth Century*.

More, Lichtheim and Hobsbawm spread their history thinner than Judt: Lichtheim covered Europe from 1900 to 1970, in 500 pages; Hobsbawm covered the world from 1914 to 1991 in 600. Judt went a step further; he wrote on Europe from 1945 to 1991 in 800 pages. *The Age of Extremes* and *Europe in the Twentieth Century* also read like a series of interlocking essays, while Judt's *Postwar* goes into much more detail: in terms of both its length and depth, it could stand as a mini encyclopedia of Europe in the period.

NOTES

1   Tony Judt, *Postwar: A History of Europe since 1945* (New York: Penguin, 2005), 10.

2   Tony Judt with Timothy Snyder, *Thinking the Twentieth Century* (London: Penguin, 2012), 283.

3   See John Gillingham, *European Integration, 1950–2003: Superstate or New Market Economy?* (Cambridge: Cambridge University Press, 2003).

4   See John Lewis Gaddis, *The Long Peace: Inquiries into the History of the Cold War* (Oxford: Oxford University Press, 1987).

5   Geoff Eley, "Europe after 1945," *History Workshop Journal* 65 (2008): 195.

6   See Denis Kozlov, "Athens and Apocalypse: Writing History in the Soviet Union," in *Oxford History of Historical Writing: 1945 to the Present* (Oxford: Oxford University Press, 2011), ed. Daniel Woolf and Axel Schneider, 375–98.

7   Jussi M. Hanhimäki and Odd Arne Westad, *The Cold War: A History in Documents and Eyewitness Accounts* (Oxford: Oxford University Press, 2003), xiii–xv.

8   Tony Judt, *Reappraisals: Reflections on the Forgotten Twentieth Century* (London: William Heinemann, 2008), 116–28.

9   Eric Hobsbawm, *The Age of Extremes: The Sort Twentieth Century, 1914– 1991* (London: Michael Joseph, 1994), 320–585.

10 Judt with Snyder, *Thinking the Twentieth Century*, 149.

11 Tony Judt, *Marxism and the French Left: Studies on Labour and Politics in France, 1830–1981* (Oxford: Oxford University Press, 1986).

12 Judt with Snyder, *Thinking the Twentieth Century*, 200.

13 Eric Hobsbawm, "After the Cold War," *London Review of Books* 34, no. 8 (April 26, 2012): 14.

14 Judt with Snyder, *Thinking the Twentieth Century*, 155.

15 Judt, *Reappraisals*, 116–28.

MODULE 4
THE AUTHOR'S CONTRIBUTION

KEY POINTS

- Judt argued that postwar European history saw Eastern and Western Europeans playing out the consequences of World War II* in the years 1945–89.

- Judt's central thesis, which probed the continuing influence of the war, gave an ordering principle to his narrative of European history that followed 1945.

- Though Judt's interest in the postwar period was not new, his insistence on the continuing influence of World War II was original.

Author's Aims

In *Postwar: A History of Europe since 1945*, Tony Judt considers the political, cultural, social, and economic history of both Eastern and Western European countries across 50 years. Given the impressive geographical, political, and chronological range of *Postwar*—from "theocratic" Ireland to communist* Bulgaria, from Soviet* Russia to Portugal in the years of dictatorship—Judt risked failing to impose a narrative on his material ("theocratic" here refers to a system of government in which religious thought plays a deciding role). In this light, his determination to combine East and West and communist and democratic Europe was particularly courageous.

That said, the book works in narrative terms, being tied together by Judt's conviction that Europe saw Eastern and Western Europeans playing out the consequences of World War II in the years 1945–91.[1] By concentrating on this event that had massively affected all of Europe (even neutral states), Judt produced a surprising, coherent

> ❝ [The] history of the two halves of post-war Europe [East and West] cannot be told in isolation from one another ... the whole of Europe lived for many decades after 1945 in the long shadow cast by the dictators and wars in its immediate past. ❞
>
> Tony Judt, *Postwar: A History of Europe since 1945*

book establishing the importance of World War II in explaining the period that followed it and proving the necessity of studying Western and Eastern Europe together.

Very rapidly after the text's publication these points moved from being incidental "extras" to crucial "givens" in an emerging field.

Approach

As historians have long appreciated, narrative histories vary in style. Does the historian choose to adopt a traditional historical narrative (sometimes called "event history")?[2] This favors "great men and women" and leading institutions, while respecting strict chronological order. Or does the historian instead choose a more modern historical narrative style? This typically means that the historian takes an interest in social and cultural changes and abandons a strict chronology; the "story" in this case unfolds not as a series of connected chronological events, but rather as a series of "snapshots" that show different aspects of the past.[3]

In the case of *Postwar*, the answer is nuanced and the book is hybrid in narrative style. Some chapters use a traditional narrative history, as when Judt's describes Britain and France's mismanagement of the 1956 Suez Crisis,* during which these countries failed to seize control of the economically and strategically important Suez Canal from the Egyptian government, and the Hungarian Rising* of 1956 against the country's dictatorial government.[4] On other occasions, though, Judt prefers modern narrative techniques, as in his pages on shifting youth culture in the 1950s and the 1960s. These address, in just a very few paragraphs, growing student numbers in European universities, the influential English pop group The Beatles,* French pop star-actor Johnny Hallyday,* London's Carnaby Street* fashion district, and the hats favored by French adolescents.[5]

This shifting focus from traditional to modern narrative and back is the inevitable consequence of *Postwar*'s broad canvas. Judt chooses the narrative style in a given part of the book on the basis of his subject matter. Yet remarkably, his rare ability to write well in so many different narrative registers allows him to deliver a book that, though tied together only by the memories of the war, boasts a basic unity.

Contribution in Context

Very few historians qualify to chronicle the experiences of a continent with a score of major languages across 50 years in different narrative techniques. Consequently, Judt had few models, save the books he mentions as an "inspiration and example" in his preface. These include Eric Hobsbawm's* *The Age of Extremes*[6] and George Lichtheim's* *Europe in the Twentieth Century*.[7]

There were precedents to Judt's attempt to tackle Europe's contemporary politics, culture, economics, and society in a single book. While previous writers had paid attention to the smaller countries, not a single one achieved Judt's level of detail or possessed his ability to switch, so convincingly, between different narrative styles. Moreover, Judt was also original in one crucial point: his thesis that the postwar period provided a long coda to World War II.

That said, some historians had previously attempted to couple different twentieth-century conflicts or to move boundaries within European history. For instance, some Cold War* historians suggest that the Cold War really began in 1917 with the Russian Revolution* that overthrew the existing monarchy, replacing it with a socialist government.[8] Judt does not claim in *Postwar* that the Cold War was an extension of World War II; rather he argues that the war touched all areas of European life, in terms of memory and consequences, up until the collapse of the Soviet bloc in 1989–91—the final act, Judt contends, of World War II.[9] This forms the driving idea behind *Postwar* and very much represents Judt's own take on later twentieth-century European history.

NOTES

1 Tony Judt, *Postwar: A History of Europe since 1945* (New York: Penguin, 2005), 6.

2 Peter Burke, "The History of Events and the Revival of Narrative," in *New Perspectives on Historical Writing*, ed. Peter Burke (University Park, PA: Penn State University Press, 1992), 233.

3 Burke, "The History of Events," 243.

4 Judt, *Postwar*, 294–302.

5 Judt, *Postwar*, 390–98.

6 Eric Hobsbawm, *Age of Extremes: The Short Twentieth Century, 1914–1991* (London: Michael Joseph, 1994).

7 George Lichtheim, *Europe in the Twentieth Century* (London: Cardinal, 1974)

8 Donald E. Davis and Eugene P. Trani, *The First Cold War: The Legacy of Woodrow Wilson in US–Soviet Relations* (Columbia, MO: University of Missouri Press, 2002), *passim.*

9 Judt, *Postwar*, 9–10.

SECTION 2
IDEAS

MODULE 5
MAIN IDEAS

KEY POINTS

- Tony Judt's key themes in *Postwar* include communal memory, the governmental system of social democracy,* and Europe's uneasy relations with superpowers.

- In *Postwar*, Judt argues that World War II* is central to understanding the history of Eastern and Western Europe in the years 1945 to 1989.

- *Postwar* is written in an accessible fashion and enjoyed a great deal of success among the general public.

Key Themes

Tony Judt's *Postwar: A History of Europe since 1945* centers on the "long shadow" cast by World War II: the way in which both Eastern and Western Europe took decades to digest the events of 1939–45. Europe only found true freedom from World War II, Judt argues, when the Soviet* bloc collapsed (1989–91).[1]

The most important of the themes fueling Judt's narrative is his analysis of European communal memory. Judt shows particular interest in selective memories of the war among affected communities: the way some memories of traumatic events were distorted or ignored, such as Nazi* reprisals against civilians ("Nazi" here refers to the extreme right-wing Nazi Party whose governance took Germany to World War II).

Another important subject involves what Judt calls "the European model"[2]—social democracy and the provision of a welfare state.* Judt links social democracy to European integration*—the attempt to unite Europe's different nations under a single continental authority.

❝ Western Europeans wanted the US to involve itself in European affairs after 1945—but they also resented that involvement and what it implied about Europe's decline. ❞

Tony Judt, *Postwar: A History of Europe since 1945*

A third key topic is Europe's ambivalent relationship with the period's superpowers: the United States for nations of Western Europe and the Soviet Union for the states of Eastern and Central Europe.

Together, these themes form the thesis that selective communal memory (a shared decision regarding what to remember and what to forget), social democracy, European integration, and superpower relations are all best understood as strategies to deal with the war's consequences.

Exploring the Ideas

Throughout *Postwar*, Judt notes the ways Europeans have remembered World War II—or in many cases have chosen to forget wartime events. As an example, Judt points to the way France and Italy tried to expunge the memories of failures against the Nazis by celebrating national resistance* movements, even though they often proved only marginally important in military terms.[3]

Judt also points to Germany's determination in the 1950s and 1960s to forget the painful events of the war, and how this gradually changed as a new generation examined the Holocaust,* not least as a way to criticize their parents.[4] World War II was remembered, then, not in a straightforward fashion but according to present needs, which varied from country to country across Europe.

Judt also describes social democracy as a "distinctive vision" of postwar Europe.[5] Its roots are to be found in prewar socialist parties, but after the war much of the center and moderate right adopted social democracy as part of a postwar consensus.*[6] Judt points here to the importance of the large-scale economic intervention of states in the war as responsible for its popularity: civil servants became used to the idea that the state should intervene in the market to safeguard national interests.[7]

Judt sees a clear connection between social democracy and European integration. He notes that the European nations involved in this push were, broadly speaking, social democratic, and that the movement originated in an attempt to bind European countries and boost each other's waning power. He also writes that, in the spirit of social democracy, European integration redistributed national funds from richer to poorer regions.[8]

Outside its borders, Europe filtered relations with its superpower neighbors through the memories of the war. Westerners looked, for the most part, with gratitude to the United States. The American-led liberation of continental Europe was the reason westerners were free: above all, the American army defeated the Nazis in the West. After the war, Western Europeans needed America to defend them from the Soviet threat—but they also resented their dependence on the United States.[9] Europeans scorned the "crassness" of invasive American culture and feared in particular that young Europeans would be Americanized.[10]

But the Soviet Union was more clearly resented in Eastern Europe, despite the fact that the Soviet Army liberated many of these countries from the Nazis. Until the 1950s the Soviet Union generally dictated terms within its satellites; for example, the Hungarian and Bulgarian show trials*—scripted court hearings largely conducted with the aim of entrenching state power or for internal political reasons—were planned in Moscow.[11] But from the later 1950s Eastern communist governments began to enjoy some autonomy.

Language and Expression

Though an academic, Judt wrote *Postwar* for the general reader who might have had only a limited background in European history. Judt considered himself a fine writer[12] and *Postwar* justifies this self-belief. The book is accessible, often witty, and above all clear. Throughout his career, Judt showed impatience with pretentious or deliberately obscure writing, believing academic history to be abysmally written.[13] Judt instead expresses difficult subjects in the easiest possible terms. As an example, he boils down the dense French philosophy of structuralism* (a system of thought that claims none of a society's constituent elements can be understood in isolation) to just two pages.[14] He also talks freely about his own experiences. Judt shares childhood memories of London shops in the 1950s—sawdust on the floor, for example—to illustrate how backward British retail was at that date.[15]

A number of critics have noted what they see as Judt's occasionally "dry" prose.[16] Many more commented favorably on particularly powerful parts of *Postwar*. They point to examples such as Judt's introduction, which describes Vienna as "a palimpsest of Europe's complicated, overlapping pasts"—a curtain raiser that sets the scene for the whole book.[17] He evokes the Ringstrasse, a mighty boulevard that calls to mind Vienna's past as an imperial capital. Like a pedestrian strolling through a living exhibit, Judt uses the city—its streets, its neighborhoods, and even its train stations—to explore different aspects of European history.

NOTES

1   Tony Judt, *Postwar: A History of Europe since 1945* (New York: Penguin, 2005), 9–10.

2   Judt, *Postwar*, 793.

3   Judt, *Postwar*, 33–4.

4   Judt, *Postwar*, 810–12.

5   Judt, *Postwar*, 363.

6   Judt, *Postwar*, 363.

7   Judt, *Postwar*, 68–70.

8   Judt, *Postwar*, 732.

9   Judt, *Postwar*, 97.

10 Judt, *Postwar*, 221.

11 Judt, *Postwar*, 179.

12 Peter Jukes, "Tony Judt: The Last Interview," *Prospect*, August 2010, accessed October 20, 2015, http://www.prospectmagazine.co.uk/magazine/tony-judt-interview.

13 Tony Judt, "A Clown in Regal Purple: Social History and the Historians," *History Workshop Journal* 7 (1979): 68.

14 Judt, *Postwar*, 399–401.

15 Judt, *Postwar*, 226.

16 See Dylan Riley, "Tony Judt: A Cooler Look," *New Left Review* 71 (2011): 52.

17 Judt, *Postwar*, 2.

MODULE 6
SECONDARY IDEAS

KEY POINTS

- In *Postwar* Tony Judt's secondary themes include the destruction of multicultural* societies in Eastern Europe; the decline of European power; the end of the politics of ambitious ideologies; and Euro-triumphalism (a powerfully declared belief in the potential success of the European system on the world stage).

- These secondary themes are crucial to *Postwar* and buttress the central idea of how World War II* impacted European life from 1945 to 1991.

- A key (if neglected) idea of Judt's is that European social and political systems work very well—and could become a model for the rest of the world in the not-so-distant future.

Other Ideas

Tony Judt's *Postwar: A History of Europe since 1945* features a number of secondary themes that run through the book. Judt was interested in the destruction of European multicultural societies, particularly in Central Europe, which had been torn apart first by the war and then by the postwar settlement. Minority German, Polish, Ukrainian, and Jewish populations were dispersed as the war ended, and in the years that followed, by the Soviet* authorities—which often moved them hundreds of miles to "their" countries. In the East, this produced postwar states with generally uniform ethnic populations.[1]

A second minor theme centers on the decline of European power. Prior to World War I* and World War II, European states still dominated world affairs. European power waned, however, with the destruction wrought by World War II and Europe's reluctance to rearm

66 But if patriotism for Europe could find a way to reach beyond itself, to capture the spirit of Heine's idealized France, 'stretching and expanding to embrace the whole of the civilized world,' then something more was now possible. The twentieth century—America's Century—had seen Europe plunge into the abyss … In spite of the horrors of their recent past—and in large measure because of them—it was *Europeans* who were now uniquely placed to offer the world some modest advice on how to avoid repeating their own mistakes. 99

Tony Judt, *Postwar: A History of Europe since 1945*

in the postwar period. As Judt points out, this was most evident in decolonization*—the process by which the African, Asian, American, and Pacific colonies of European nations claimed their independence; through either choice or force, Belgium, Britain, France, the Netherlands, Portugal and Spain withdrew from their colonial possessions from the late 1940s through the 1970s.[2]

A third minor theme involves what Judt calls "the withering away of the 'master narratives' of European history."[3] Big ideas— most spectacularly communism,* nationalism* (belief in a nation's primacy, sometimes founded on racist mythologizing) and classical liberalism* (the belief that the state should intervene as little as possible in the market and in the life of the citizen)—became unpopular after World War II. Enthusiasm grew, particularly in the West, for systems that worked, whatever their ideological roots. Thus one consequence was a postwar consensus,* as left- and right-wing parties scrambled to occupy the middle ground. With the exception of the Italian and French Communist Parties, extremist organizations had little electoral success in the Western half of the continent from the 1950s to the 1980s.

Exploring the Ideas

These secondary themes link to Judt's central thesis about the long shadow of World War II. For example, the great melting pots of different peoples in the heart of Europe suffered two great blows before breaking: the actions of the Nazi* murder squads and postwar ethnic cleansing*— the forced removal or even murder of people in a region according to their ethnic descent—on the part of the Soviet authorities. In the decades that followed, Central Europe evolved from a confused ethnic mosaic into a series of ethnically defined countries.[4] The falling away of European power was, of course, intimately connected with Europe's bloodletting in the war—and meanwhile, anticolonial* movements took root in many parts of the world and had to be dealt with in the next decades;[5] "colonial" here describes the settling and exploitation of a foreign nation or people by a more powerful nation or people. The end of "the big idea," whether an extreme form of nationalism or communism, also owes much to disillusionment with the performance of these systems during World War II and in its aftermath.

The secondary themes buttress some of Judt's other important notions in *Postwar*. He cites the atrocities that led to the end of the Central European melting pot, which the new ethnic states remembered selectively.[6] The disintegration of bold ideologies such as communism also led to a broad consensus across the continent for a new politics—one that ultimately produced moderate and pragmatic social democratic systems with strong welfare* provisions.[7] Eventually, the end of European colonial power kickstarted European integration;* some countries—crucially Belgium, France, and Germany—saw this collective action as a way to counteract international decline.[8]

Overlooked

One minor theme neglected by commentators is Judt's Euro-triumphalism: that is, his belief that the European system would be successful on the world stage. As Judt charts Western Europe's rapid recovery from the war and the remarkable 30 years of growth that followed, he praises the robustness and effectiveness of European social democracy. He also gives qualified support to the movement for European integration; towards the end of *Postwar*, Judt goes even further. Looking towards the future, he writes, "Few would have predicted it 60 years before, but the twenty-first century might yet belong to Europe."[9] This implies that Europe—and not the United States—might become the natural point of reference for the world in the twenty-first century.

While some readers have noted Judt's Euro-triumphalism, it has not yet been analyzed or debated,[10] perhaps for the simple reason that Europe suffered grave economic reverses in the decade after the publication of *Postwar*. In fact, the Eurozone*—the region sharing the euro as the currency—has experienced poor growth since 1999, with the exception of Germany. The 2008 international banking crisis led quickly to the ongoing euro debt crisis,* in which certain European nations found themselves unable to repay debts at the level of the state, and the European economy has suffered since, particularly relative to the rest of the Western world. Should the European economy grow convincingly and Europe represent a credible world model once more, it is very possible that this theme in *Postwar* will attract more attention.

NOTES

1   Tony Judt, *Postwar: A History of Europe since 1945* (New York: Penguin, 2005), 24–7.

2   Judt, *Postwar*, 279–92.

3   Judt, *Postwar*, 7.

4   Judt, *Postwar*, 9.

5   See Judt, *Postwar*, 279–92.

6   Judt, *Postwar*, 26–7.

7   Judt, *Postwar*, 360–89.

8   Judt, *Postwar*, 326.

9   Judt, *Postwar*, 800.

10 Bruce Bawer, "In the Shadow of the Gulag: Tony Judt's Europe," *The Hudson Review* (2007): 694.

MODULE 7
ACHIEVEMENT

KEY POINTS

- On publication in 2005, Tony Judt's *Postwar* became an instant prize-winning classic, favorably reviewed and translated into many languages.

- The text's success can be attributed to Judt's rare ability as a narrative historian: he wrote a coherent history of a whole continent, spanning a half century—a history that appealed to both historians and the general public.

- Judt made the controversial decision not to include references or a bibliography in *Postwar* and he did not manage later to include, as he had hoped, references on the Internet.

Assessing the Argument

In *Postwar: A History of Europe since 1945*, Tony Judt achieved two remarkable feats. First, he created a unified narrative of European history that spanned 1945 to 1991 (and beyond). Second, he tied this narrative by showing the importance of World War II* in explaining postwar events. However, *Postwar* is not always unified in narrative terms—nor is it always linked to the war.

For instance, there has been some general concern that the book offers uneven narrative coverage. There are also, as it happens, clear chronological and geographical biases: Britain receives about four times more coverage than Spain, despite being only a third larger in population.[1] Likewise Judt concentrates on the immediate postwar period and the collapse of the Soviet Union* in the late 1980s. Indeed, about 300 of the book's 800 pages relate to two periods lasting together a little less than a decade: 1945–50 and 1989–91.

> **❝** [*Postwar* is Judt's] unmatched, and perhaps unmatchable, history of postwar Europe. **❞**
>
> Timothy Snyder, *Thinking the Twentieth Century*

Of course, narrative histories must make such choices: "uniform" narratives are neither possible nor desirable. Britain changed more radically from 1945 to 1970 than Spain; arguably, the years 1945–50 also matter more to European history than, say, 1955–60.

Likewise, Judt himself recognizes that his thesis for explaining postwar European history as a product of World War II is not a cast-iron rule. For example, mass immigration to the continent from Africa and Asia,[2] or the trajectory of Franco's* dictatorship in Spain,[3] are difficult to link back to the war. Yet Judt himself understood many of these imperfections while writing his "avowedly personal" take on the European past.[4] Narrative history of the kind Judt writes, by its very nature, does not easily conform to master theories—and that he recognizes this contributes to *Postwar*'s strength.

Achievement in Context

The prestigious publishing house Penguin released *Postwar* in London and New York in 2005. It excited an unusual number of major reviews on both sides of the Atlantic, most of which were overwhelmingly positive. It was shortlisted for the Pulitzer Prize* in the nonfiction category and the Samuel Johnson Prize in 2006. That same year, it captured the Arthur Ross Book Award as "an outstanding contribution to the understanding of foreign policy or international relations." In the next decade, *Postwar* was translated into French, German, Hebrew, Italian, Japanese, Spanish, Polish, and Portuguese. It has also been made into a 43-hour audio book; few nonfiction books of almost 1,000 pages are recorded in this fashion.[5]

Judt's decision not to include a bibliography and to publish reference notes on the Internet served to limit the text's academic appeal, however.[6] This controversial decision was compounded when the bibliography appeared as a long reading list rather than a reference tool,[7] while the notes have never materialized. This is particularly difficult to justify as Judt used archive material for part of the book.[8] It is possible that Judt's cancer, for which he received treatment in 2002, pushed him to hurry his work towards completion without a conventional academic apparatus.[9] He has also talked of an insistent editor pressuring him to finish the book.[10] *Postwar* is, in any case, a very unusual work: a celebrated narrative by a master historian that does not meet the most basic academic standards of referencing. This lack of a critical apparatus created unease in some readers—and was, according to one judge, a reason that *Postwar* did not win the Pulitzer Prize.[11]

Limitations

In writing *Postwar*, Judt claimed that his work was limited to half a century of European history (1945–89).[12] He generally keeps to these limits, save in his writings on the two superpowers, the United States and the "half-European" Soviet Union.[13] These powers, of course, dominated the halves of Europe through this period, and so their internal developments are necessarily part of the story. Additionally, Judt's main idea—that European history in this half century was a coda to World War II—also limits any general lessons that *Postwar* might offer. Judt very much anchors his book in a particular time and space.

While at first glance *Postwar* has few applications to other periods and other cultures, one central point concerns the way memory of the recent past is manipulated. So it should come as no surprise to learn that *Postwar* has been employed in the history of what came before (the war) and after (the current affairs of Europe in the last decade). Giving such a rich history of the remembering (and forgetting) of Nazi* extermination, Judt's work has been discussed and cited in histories of the Holocaust.*[14] Moreover, as it looked ahead to contemporary debates, *Postwar* (often coupled with its successor *Ill Fares the Land*) has starred in works on modern social democracy.*[15] This is a rare accomplishment in a historical volume: *Postwar* not only looks to the past with authority, but opens a door on the future.

NOTES

1   Tony Judt, *Postwar: A History of Europe since 1945* (New York: Penguin, 2005), 851–3, 870–1, 841–2 and 838.

2   Judt, *Postwar*, 333–7.

3   Judt, *Postwar*, 226–7.

4   Judt, *Postwar*, XIII.

5   Tony Judt, *Postwar: A History of Europe since 1945, Audiobook* (Ashland, OR: Blackstone Audio, 2011).

6   Judt, *Postwar*, XIII.

7   "Postwar Bibliography," accessed November 1, 2015, http://remarque. as.nyu.edu/docs/IO/9076/PostwarBibliography.pdf.

8   Michael Freund, "A History of Two Europes" (interview with Judt), *The Vienna Review*, October 1, 2006, accessed October 20, 2006, http://www. viennareview.net/vienna-review-book-reviews/upcoming-literary-events/a-history-of-two-europes.

9   Jennifer Homans, "Introduction: In Good Faith," in Tony Judt, *When The Facts Change: Essays 1995–2010* (London: William Heinemann, 2015), 3.

10 Freund, "A History."

11 Patton Stacey, "Wait, Your Footnotes Are in Cyberspace?," August 18, 2014, accessed October 20, 2015, https://chroniclevitae.com/news/665–wait-your-footnotes-are-in-cyberspace.

12 Judt, *Postwar*, 1–10.

13 Judt, *Postwar*, 7.

14 Peter Hayes, *How Was It Possible? A Holocaust Reader* (Lincoln, NE: University of Nebraska Press, 2015), 801–20.

15 Tony Judt, *Ill Fares the Land* (London: Allen Lane, 2010); Jack Luzkow, *The Great Forgetting: The Past, Present and Future of Social Democracy and the Welfare State* (Manchester: Manchester University Press, 2015).

MODULE 8
PLACE IN THE AUTHOR'S WORK

KEY POINTS

- Prior to *Postwar,* Tony Judt had specialized in French political and intellectual history.

- The text marked a departure for Judt as he moved from partial histories of France to a general account that spanned 50 years of European history.

- *Postwar* completed a transformation in Tony Judt's reputation: a British historian writing on French political history became a historian with continental ambitions.

Positioning

Tony Judt published *Postwar: A History of Europe since 1945* in 2005. At this date he was a leading figure among contemporary historians, the director (and founder) of the Erich Maria Remarque Institute* (an institution in New York dedicated to the study of contemporary Europe), and a regular essayist for American and British periodicals. His success was based in large part on his publications: he had produced scores of articles[1] and edited, with other scholars, four collections of essays.[2] He had also authored six books on modern and contemporary European history,[3] five of which concerned the history of left-wing movements in nineteenth- and twentieth-century France. Two titles give a sense of their narrow focus: *Socialism in Provence 1871–1914; Past Imperfect: French Intellectuals, 1944–1956.*

Postwar is different though. Its 800 pages cover not just a few years of one country's past but, rather, half a century of Western and Eastern European history. Widely and immediately acclaimed, the book marked the arrival of Tony Judt as a contemporary historian admired

❝ [*Postwar*] is clearly the book of a British man with Eastern European roots, of a baby-boomer, a beneficiary of the welfare principle, and someone with a strong interest in the French history of ideas. **❞**

Tony Judt in an interview with Michael Freund

by his peers and as what he has called elsewhere "a public intellectual."[4] Indeed, Judt's working-class parents only realized their son's importance with the success he gained through *Postwar*.[5]

Integration

Although Judt's early written focus on France had always cloaked a much wider interest in contemporary European history, this did not emerge into print beyond a number of articles. Still, we can trace an evolution within Judt's published books. Judt's first three works offered careful, forensic examinations of the history of the French left: the first and third (published in 1976 and 1990) concentrated on political history; the second, *Socialism in Provence* (1979), looked instead at the social and economic background of the Socialist* Party in southern France. From there, Judt wrote two histories of left-wing thought in France, looking at thinkers who in his view were seduced by Soviet* communism* in *Past Imperfect* (1992) and those who resisted in *The Burden of Responsibility* (1998). These books demonstrated his ability to write intellectual history.

The Burden of Responsibility was written and published while Judt was researching *Postwar*, and left its mark on that book. Also while working on *Postwar*, Judt published *A Grand Illusion?* (1996), an extended essay on European integration.* This was his first book not exclusively on France and the first clue (together with some 1990s articles) that Judt had turned to other, more ambitious projects. The arguments of *A Grand Illusion?* would be absorbed in part by *Postwar*.

Judt was struck down with a serious neurological condition in 2008, just three years after the publication of *Postwar*.[6] The diagnosis of this degenerative illness, amyotrophic lateral sclerosis,* both concentrated and directed Judt's interest into several personal works, all of which touch on themes developed in *Postwar*. These were: *Reappraisals* (a collection of essays); *The Memory Chalet* (2010, a personal but very historically minded memoir); and *Ill Fares the Land* (2010, a despairing defense of social democracy). Judt died of his illness in 2010 and two posthumous works were also published: *Thinking the Twentieth Century* (2012 autobiographical sketches mixed with conversations with the historian Timothy Snyder),* and a second collection of essays, *When the Facts Change* (2015).

Significance

Postwar stands out among Judt's published works; longer and more ambitious than any of his other books, it focuses on a continent rather than a country and spanned 15 years from conception to publication. The works on France showed an author who alternated between cultural, political, economic, and social history. In *Postwar*, Judt synthesized these interests for maximum impact.

Evidence of Judt's earlier interests appears in the subject matter of *Postwar*. Judt chose to cover the history of Western and Eastern Europe—and for Eastern Europe particularly, but also for western intellectuals looking east, a good understanding of communist thought was absolutely essential to succeed at this task. Judt had become a world expert on this subject in his five books on French leftist movements, particularly in *Past Imperfect* and *The Burden of Responsibility*. Not surprisingly, his treatments of Western communist supporters such as Jean-Paul Sartre* and internal debates in Eastern communist governments were superlative.[7]

Judt's autobiographical sketches in *The Memory Chalet*, his discussions of history with Timothy Snyder, and some of his essays, mostly depended on *Postwar*. Indeed, it is unlikely that any of these books would have been published had *Postwar* not made it into print and attracted the public's interest. In fact, they are best seen as appendices where Judt is still thinking out the problems he addressed in *Postwar*. The book *Ill Fares the Land*, for example, clearly builds on his social democratic* writings in *Postwar*. Judt in this instance turns from narrative history to political polemic (a vehemently argued position): it is a work that can be understood as a variation on a powerful theme.

NOTES

1   Tony Judt, *When The Facts Change: Essays 1995–2010* (London: William Heinemann, 2015), 367–73.

2   Tony Judt, ed., *Resistance and Revolution in Mediterranean Europe 1939– 1948* (London: Routledge, 1989); Tony Judt and Denis Lacorne, eds., *With Us or Against Us: Studies in Global Anti-Americanism* (Basingstoke: Palgrave Macmillan, 2005); István Deák, Jan T. Gross, and Tony Judt, eds., *The Politics of Retribution in Europe: World War II and its Aftermath* (Princeton, NJ: Princeton University Press, 2000); Tony Judt and Denis Lacorne, eds., *Language, Nation, and State: Identity Politics in a Multilingual Age* (Basingstoke: Palgrave Macmillan, 2004).

3   Tony Judt, *La reconstruction du Parti Socialiste, 1920–26* (Paris: Fondation nationale des sciences politiques, 1976); Tony Judt, *Socialism in Provence, 1871–1914: A Study in the Origins of the Modern French Left* (Cambridge: Cambridge University Press, 1979); Tony Judt, *Marxism and the French Left: Studies on Labour and Politics in France, 1830–1981* (Oxford: Oxford University Press, 1986); Tony Judt, *Past Imperfect: French Intellectuals, 1944–1956* (Berkeley, CA: University of California Press, 1992); Tony Judt, *A Grand Illusion? An Essay on Europe* (New York: Hill and Wang, 1996); Tony Judt, *The Burden of Responsibility: Blum, Camus, Aron, and the French Twentieth Century* (Chicago, IL: University of Chicago Press, 1998).

4   Tony Judt, *Reappraisals: Reflections on the Forgotten Twentieth Century* (London: William Heinemann, 2008), 164.

5   Tony Judt with Timothy Snyder, *Thinking the Twentieth Century* (London: Penguin, 2012), 153.

6   Tony Judt, *The Memory Chalet* (London: William Heinemann, 2010), 15–21.

7   Tony Judt, *Postwar: A History of Europe since 1945* (New York: Penguin, 2005), 401–7, 426–36.

SECTION 3
IMPACT

MODULE 9
THE FIRST RESPONSES

KEY POINTS

- *Postwar* has been criticized for its leftist bias and its analysis of social democracy.*

- Although Tony Judt did not answer these criticisms directly, he did defend the writing of "opinionated" history in a later work.

- Readers seem to have been more impressed with the extraordinary detail and range of *Postwar* than the criticisms raised against it.

Criticism

Tony Judt's *Postwar: A History of Europe since 1945* was published in 2005 to great acclaim. Here was a narrative history of a period that historians had covered in little depth. Nor was the book's central thesis—the primacy of World War II* in subsequent European affairs—particularly controversial. However, criticisms emerged in and among the congratulatory reviews and most came down to two points: bias and political science.

First, a number of reviewers claimed that *Postwar* offered a leftist version of recent European history, and therefore a one-sided narrative. While Judt consistently criticized the Soviet Union,* Norman Davies* (a British historian and specialist on Poland) suggested that Judt was reluctant "to give the Stalinist spade its real name."[1] Historian Gregor Dallas went further and accused Judt of being an unrepentant Marxist* whose "rug was pulled from under his feet" by the collapse of communism* in 1989–91.[2] The American polemicist Bruce Bawer,* meanwhile, attacked Judt for overlooking the "Islamization"

> **"** A masterpiece of historical scholarship. *Postwar* gives us a view of Europe over the past 60 years in which east and west, culture and geopolitics are seamlessly interwoven. **"**
>
> John Gray, Review in *The Independent*

of Europe, "the major shortcoming of the book"[3] ("polemicist" here refers to a writer of forcefully put arguments).

In *Postwar*, Judt wrote extensively on social democracy as a particularly European social model. Here, too, the right attacked Judt as a defender of statist solutions (that is, solutions to social problems in which the state is the principal actor).[4] Concerns also came from the left, however; the leftist American sociologist* Dylan Riley claimed that Judt misunderstood the agricultural background that led to Scandinavian social democracy.[5] In addition, Riley derided Judt's notion that European integration* had amounted to a form of social democracy.[6]

Responses

Tony Judt did not respond directly to the criticisms made of *Postwar*. In fact, Judt makes only one reference to a review in all his subsequent writings. In 2010, he described his satisfaction at how Norman Davies—with whom Judt had a chilly relationship—had generally complimented *Postwar* in the British newspaper the *Guardian*. "This is history-writing with a human face, as well as with brainpower ... it is most unlikely that Judt's achievement will be superseded soon."[7]

Judt was apparently indifferent to criticisms of bias. After all, he had been very clear that *Postwar* was "an avowedly personal interpretation of the recent European past"[8] and returned to this in a later publication where he defended his right to publish "opinionated" history.[9] As it happened, most conservative reviewers accepted this position as an honest one: Judt had certainly never attempted to hide his political views.

In one area Judt continued to evolve in his thinking, taking forward the social democratic theme. Judt dictated *Ill Fares the Land* in 2010, as he was dying, but it is difficult to know whether he was reacting to criticisms of *Postwar* or to other stimuli. Regardless, he painted a far more pessimistic picture about the future of social democracy than in *Postwar*. However, he was also more strident in his own support for that political system than had been possible in his narrative history.

It is likely that Judt would eventually have revised *Postwar*—not least because so much happened in Europe immediately after its publication. The problem with contemporary history is that it keeps happening and perspectives on the past inevitably change. Judt's early death meant that he never had the chance to bring out a new edition; as a result, even elementary factual mistakes have remained.

Conflict and Consensus

Warmly reviewed in 2005 and 2006, *Postwar* has quickly become a classic of contemporary history and regularly appears in academic and popular works on Europe. Criticisms of the book have not proven particularly durable; certainly they have not damaged the reputation of either author or book. Judt's premature death means *Postwar* will remain in its present form: even if permission were granted, revising the book without the author's input would take a superhuman effort.

Much of the enthusiasm over *Postwar* stemmed from its range. While there is no question that Judt's achievement was remarkable when the book was published in 2005, other books have since emerged with a similar range. Three works from British historians stand out in this respect: Tom Buchanan's* *Europe's Troubled Peace, 1945–2000* (2005), Bernard Wasserstein's* *Barbarism and Civilization: A History of Europe in our Time* (2009), and Dan Stone's* *Goodbye to All That? The Story of Europe since 1945* (2014).[10] Thus one thing that made *Postwar* so unusual—the lack of narrative histories covering postwar Europe—has become less remarkable. Even so, the very fact that these books follow Judt's model so closely, Stone's in particular, testifies to *Postwar*'s ultimate success.

NOTES

1   Norman Davies, "The New European Century," Guardian, December 3, 2005, accessed November 1, 2015, http://www.theguardian.com/books/2005/dec/03/featuresreviews.guardianreview4.

2   Gregor Dallas, "Tony Judt: Historian of the Postwar Age," *GD-Frontiers* (2005 [requested for *Literary Review* but then refused by the same]), accessed November 1, 2015, http://www.gd-frontiers.net/spip.php?article11.

3   Bruce Bawer, "In the Shadow of the Gulag: Tony Judt's Europe," *The Hudson Review* (2007): 698–9.

4   Bawer, "Shadow," 690.

5   Dylan Riley, "Tony Judt: A Cooler Look," *New Left Review* 71 (2011): 53–4.

6   Riley, "Tony Judt," 56.

7   Davies, "The New European Century"; Tony Judt with Timothy Snyder, *Thinking the Twentieth Century* (London: Penguin, 2012), 254.

8   Judt, *Postwar*, XIII.

9   Judt with Snyder, *Thinking the Twentieth Century*, 396.

10 Tom Buchanan, *Europe's Troubled Peace: 1945 to the Present* (London: Wiley-Blackwell, 2005); Bernard Wasserstein, *Barbarism and Civilization: A History of Europe in our Time* (Oxford: Oxford University Press, 2009); Dan Stone, *Goodbye to All That? The Story of Europe since 1945* (Oxford: Oxford University Press, 2014).

MODULE 10
THE EVOLVING DEBATE

KEY POINTS

- In *Postwar,* Judt created the idea of a unified European period of history stretching from 1945 to 1991, incorporating East and West, and independent of the history of the United States and the Soviet Union.*

- Judt helped create a territory within his discipline that ever-larger numbers of historians are exploiting.

- Judt's natural successor might be the historian Timothy Snyder* of the United States, coauthor of *Thinking the Twentieth Century* (2012).

Uses and Problems

Tony Judt's *Postwar: A History of Europe since 1945* today stands as the classic account of Cold War* European history. It would be difficult to write an essay, never mind a book, on any part of Europe's postwar period through 1991 without including Judt. Consider recent works on postwar Scandinavia, where Judt's name appears as a point of reference, notably in a recent discussion of Scandinavia's future in Europe.[1] Judt also appears in a discussion of Norway's foreign policy[2] and in another on Scandinavia's foreign relations generally.[3] *Postwar* is referenced in the same way for most regions of Europe—particularly Western Europe. The text's status as an important landmark for contemporary historians was secure a decade after its publication.

Judt's legacy has progressed beyond influencing the scholarship of postwar Europe, however. Judt is much quoted by historians of the Holocaust*[4] for his final chapter on the ways in which the memory of the murder of Jewish Europeans has been manipulated;[5] indeed, Judt's

❝ ... I read [*Postwar*] primarily as a wake-up call, reminding Europeans of a period in which they responded to a self-inflicted catastrophe by forming new alliances, restructuring institutions and adopting long-term solutions. Is it necessary to have a war to generate such energy? ❞

Mark Mazower, Review in *New Statesman*

work on memory has been used in several other contexts where clashes are remembered selectively—including, for example, the Palestinian conflict.[6]

Postwar remains, then, a text of the very first importance for contemporary history. Yet Judt also remains influential in terms of his central idea that the war and its memory animated Europe's postwar period. This idea has become central in the work of other writers including, most notably, the British professor Dan Stone.*[7] In *Goodbye to All That? The Story of Europe since 1945* (2015), Stone sums up Europe's history in terms Judt would have applauded: "The impact of the Second World War ... did not end in 1945. Without understanding the nature of the Second World War, one cannot get to grips with what followed."[8]

Schools of Thought

As a professor at New York University and head of the Erich Maria Remarque Institute* in New York, an institution whose purpose lies in research in contemporary European history, Tony Judt came into contact with a series of gifted young historians; he had, in fact, a reputation for helping junior members of the profession.[9] With *Postwar*, Judt published the single most influential work on Cold War Europe. All the preconditions for a "school of thought" coalescing around him were ripe. But no such thing happened, perhaps because of the text's nature; while it is a sophisticated narrative history, its central thesis that the effects of World War II* lasted for almost half a century is not likely to lead to arguments among competing groups of historians.

If anything, readers are more likely to draw inspiration from Judt's approach to the history of Eastern and Western Europe and his mining of different kinds of history to create a particular space within the discipline. Judt treats postwar Europe as an independent whole, not just as an annex to American or Soviet history, and few historians had previously studied this space free of other concerns; the few who took on postwar Europe had focused on European integration* or the Cold War. But thanks to Judt and others like him, including Alan Milward* and Eric Hobsbawm,* "postwar" became a subject of study in its own right and in the last 10 years, a new generation of historians has probed that space deeper.

In Current Scholarship

In many ways the American historian Timothy Snyder is a natural successor to Tony Judt. The two met while Snyder was a young graduate, and Judt spoke to Snyder weekly while the young scholar prepared his controversial book *Bloodlands: Europe between Hitler and Stalin.*[10] Judt was at this point terminally ill and, with his permission, Snyder recorded their conversations in *Thinking the Twentieth Century*, published in 2012, two years after Judt's death.[11]

Thinking the Twentieth Century reveals a bond between these men founded on a shared passion for Eastern and Western Europe (and a knowledge of the relevant languages), a conviction in the importance of intellectual and political history, leftist politics founded on a hostility to Soviet politics, and a particular interest in the ways in which the Holocaust was conducted and remembered).[12]

Since Judt's death, Snyder has continued to write about the atrocities of World War II, publishing an ambitious study in 2015, *Black*

Earth: The Holocaust as History and Warning. Above all, Snyder reveals a strong commitment, like Judt before him, towards a "good history" where societies encounter their own past—however painful the experience.[13]

NOTES

1   Thorsten Borring Olesen, "A Nordic Sonderweg to Europe: Integration History from a Northern Perspective," in *Northern Europe and the Future of the EU*, ed. Helge Hoibraaten and Jochen Hille (Cambridge: Intersentia, 2011), 36–7.

2   James Larry Taulbee, Ann Kelleher, Peter C. Grosvenor, *Norway's Peace Policy: Soft Power in a Turbulent World* (New York: Palgrave Macmillan, 2014), 32.

3   Mary Hilson, *The Nordic Model: Scandinavia since 1945* (London: Reaktion, 2008), 124.

4   See Peter Hayes, *How Was It Possible? A Holocaust Reader* (Lincoln, NE: University of Nebraska Press, 2015), 801–20; David Cesarani, "Introduction," in *After the Holocaust*, ed. David Cesarani and Eric Sundquist (Abingdon: Routledge, 2012), 13.

5   Tony Judt, *Postwar: A History of Europe since 1945* (New York: Penguin, 2005), 803–31.

6   Menachem Klein, *Lives in Common: Arabs and Jews in Jerusalem, Jaffa and Hebron* (London: Hurst & Co., 2014).

7   Dan Stone, *Goodbye to All That? The Story of Europe since 1945* (Oxford: Oxford University Press, 2014), xi.

8   Stone, *Goodbye*, 3.

9   Tony Judt with Timothy Snyder, *Thinking the Twentieth Century* (London: Penguin, 2012), xv.

10 Timothy Synder, *Bloodlands: Europe between Hitler and Stalin* (New York: Basic Books, 2010), 420.

11 Judt with Snyder, *Thinking the Twentieth Century*.

12 Judt with Snyder, *Thinking the Twentieth Century*, 392.

13 Judt with Snyder, *Thinking the Twentieth Century*, 259–83.

MODULE 11
IMPACT AND INFLUENCE TODAY

KEY POINTS

- *Postwar* has emerged as the only truly convincing history of Europe in the period between the end of World War II* and the collapse of the Soviet* bloc.

- At the end of his life, Judt published a work which emerged from his research in *Postwar, Ill Fares the Land* (2010), in which he defended the efficacy of the governmental system of social democracy.*

- Judt's *Ill Fares the Land* is much more overtly political than *Postwar* and has been quoted in a series of political tracts.

Position

Tony Judt's *Postwar: A History of Europe since 1945* has proven immensely influential in the field of contemporary European history. The name of Judt's work is echoed, for example, in the title of the recent *Oxford Handbook of Postwar European History* (2012), a collection of essays on the period he made his own; had it had been published a decade before, the Oxford volume would probably have been called the *Oxford Handbook of Cold War European History*. Its editor, Dan Stone,* employed Judt's chronological divisions from *Postwar*, judging these the most useful available.[1] Judt also appears 14 times in the index—making him by far, in terms of citation, the most influential historian in the work.[2] In these 14 appearances, only one of Stone's authors takes issue with Judt, and then only partially;[3] the others quote him approvingly.

Contemporary historians have embraced *Postwar* in large part because of its remarkable depth and range. While it contains many carefully argued passages, among them Judt's reflection on the

> **❝** Something is profoundly wrong with the way we live today. For thirty years we have made a virtue out of the pursuit of material self-interest … We know what things cost but have no idea what they are worth. We no longer ask of a judicial ruling or a legislative act: Is it good? Is it fair? Is it just? Is it right? Will it help bring about a better society or a better world? Those used to be the political questions even if they invited no easy answers. We must learn once again to pose them. **❞**
>
> Tony Judt, *Ill Fares the Land*

importance of the Holocaust* in European memory,[4] it can also stand, with its excellent index, as a reference guide for the crucial postwar period of European history. Indeed, *Postwar*'s lasting importance will perhaps depend not so much on Judt's arguments or asides, but on his creation of a well-defined period and area that deserve the attention of historians. As such, *Postwar* serves to define an emergent territory in the field of history.

Interaction

If scholars did not see *Postwar* itself as particularly controversial, Judt's spin-off project—*Ill Fares the Land* (2010)—sparked much more debate. In *Postwar* Judt argued that social democracy was a characteristically European form of government.[5] His discussion was clearly impassioned and self-admittedly partisan; for example, he attacked British prime minister Margaret Thatcher,* noted for her controversial governance in the 1980s, whom he viewed as an enemy of social democracy.[6] While conservative reviewers noted Judt's position here with irritation, none felt that it fatally detracted from the book's value.[7]

Remarkably, Judt took on this project as he was dying. He completed *Ill Fares the Land*, a vehement political statement rather than a narrative history, five years after *Postwar*. In it Judt argued that social democracy represented the best system available for Europe— and by implication the rest of the world—but that it was threatened by a neoliberal* consensus ("neoliberalism" here refers to the political ideology that governments must not intervene in the workings of the market, even at the expense of welfare provisions for a society's most vulnerable). He borrowed data and graphics from the British scholars Richard Wilkinson* and Kate Pickett,* authors of *The Spirit Level: Why Greater Equality Makes Societies Stronger*,[8] to argue that market capitalism,* the social and economic system dominant in the West (and increasingly throughout the rest of the world) creates too much inequality.[9] Judt urged the young to defend social democracy, suggesting useful arguments to that end.[10]

The Continuing Debate

A text owing much to *Postwar*, *Ill Fares the Land* inspired (or helped to inspire) a series of works defending social democracy, including several notable leftist publications, some of which were academic. For example, Jack Luzkow's* 2015 book *The Great Forgetting: The Past, Present and Future of Social Democracy and the Welfare State*[11] is dedicated to Judt. Political books and pamphlets also quoted Judt approvingly, including *Left Without a Future* (a 2013 analysis that hopes for the revival of British social democracy),[12] and *All That's Left* (a 2010 book on the hope for a revival of the left in Australia).[13] Even popular English-language books on political economy approved Judt, including the second edition of the British social scientist Danny Dorling's* *Injustice: Why Social Inequality Still Persists*.[14] There are few signs, however, that *Ill Fares the Land* has inspired readers outside the English-speaking world.

It will be interesting to see whether *Ill Fares the Land* brings a new political readership to *Postwar*. As noted above, Judt always made his leftist affiliations clear. And even in the context of *Postwar's* narrative history, his defense of social democracy sometimes worried his more conservative readers.[15] Understandably, the response from the right to *Ill Fares the Land* was more strident than the reactions to *Postwar*. For instance, the British Conservative Chris Patten* attacked Judt's "romantic view of the world,"[16] while Josef Joffe,* writing in the *New York Times*, compared the American to the European model and concluded, "It is still easier to escape from the slums of America than from the *banlieues** of France"[17] (the *banlieues* being poor urban areas ringing major French cities).

NOTES

1 Dan Stone, "The Editor's Introduction," in *The Oxford Handbook of Postwar European History*, ed. Dan Stone (Oxford: Oxford University Press, 2012), 10–11.

2 Stone, *Handbook*, 750.

3 Samuel Moyn, "Intellectuals and Nazism," in *The Oxford Handbook of Postwar European History*, ed. Dan Stone (Oxford: Oxford University Press, 2012), 688.

4 Tony Judt, *Postwar: A History of Europe since 1945* (New York: Penguin, 2005), 803–31.

5 Judt, *Postwar*, 363.

6 Judt, *Postwar*, 539–47.

7 See Bruce Bawer, "In the Shadow of the Gulag: Tony Judt's Europe," *The Hudson Review* (2007): 690.

8 Richard Wilkinson and Kate Pickett, *The Spirit Level: Why Greater Equality Makes Societies Stronger* (London: Bloomsbury Press, 2009).

9 Tony Judt, *Ill Fares the Land* (London: Allen Lane, 2010), 15–16.

10 Judt, *Ill Fares*, 237.

11 Jack Luzkow, *The Great Forgetting: The Past, Present and Future of Social Democracy and the Welfare State* (Manchester: Manchester University Press, 2015).

12 Anthony Painter, *Left Without a Future: Social Justice in Anxious Times* (London: Taurus 2013), 14–15, 18, 64.

13 Nick Dyrenfurth and Tim Soutphommasane, eds., *All That's Left: What Labor Should Stand For* (Sydney: University of New South Wales Press, 2010), 7, 51 and 54.

14 Danny Dorling, *Injustice: Why Social Inequality Still Persists* (Bristol: Policy Press, 2015), 377–8.

15 See Daniel Johnson, "Postwar by Tony Judt," *Commentary*, October 1, 2005, accessed October 20, 2015, https://www.commentarymagazine.com/articles/postwar-by-tony-judt/.

16 Chris Patten, "Ill Fares the Land," *Guardian*, April 11, 2010, accessed November 1, 2015, http://www.theguardian.com/books/2010/apr/11/ill-fares-land-tony-judt.

17 Josef Joffe, "The Worst of the West," *New York Times*, April 30, 2010, accessed November 1, 2015, http://www.nytimes.com/2010/05/02/books/review/Joffe-t.html?_r=0.

MODULE 12
WHERE NEXT?

KEY POINTS

- *Postwar*'s future status will depend, as in all books about the recent past, on the direction the discipline of history now takes.

- *Postwar* will inspire future studies covering both Eastern and Western Europe, though these are likely to cover shorter periods of history.

- *Postwar* remains our best history of all of Europe—East and West, large and small countries—in the period between the surrender of Nazi* Germany (1945) and the collapse of Soviet* communism* (1989–91).

Potential

Tony Judt's *Postwar: A History of Europe since 1945* is a much-celebrated work of recent scholarship. Its future success is likely to depend on two factors. First, *Postwar* was written very soon after the final events it described. As Eric Hobsbawm* noted in his tribute to Judt following his death, our view of the text might become more critical as the years pass and we get a better perspective on the Europe that Judt described.[1] For example, some of his enthusiasm for European integration* (written just after the introduction of the euro, the single European currency) is rather jarring to those familiar with, and affected by, the ongoing euro debt crisis;* for many months in 2015, for example, Greece threatened to withdraw from the single currency altogether.[2] If that crisis worsens, much of that part of *Postwar* will ring hollow. But if the European economy returns to previous levels of growth, these portions will read much more convincingly.

❝ *Postwar* covers a great deal of ground; but the unapologetically grand narrative at its center was a record in the end of sane, modest, and intelligible political success, and the life chances which that success made possible. That is not how the continent looks today, nor alas how it really is. It takes a very sanguine temperament for the present not to fear that the pusillanimous, myopic and muddled agency and inertia of its current politicians now jeopardize much of the achievement Tony wished to celebrate. ❞

John Dunn, "Tony Judt's Twentieth Century"

Second, Judt wrote *Postwar* at a time when it was one of very few books describing Eastern and Western Cold War* Europe. This is now changing though and readers have other options, including Tom Buchanan's* *Europe's Troubled Peace, 1945–2000* (2005) and Bernard Wasserstein's* *Barbarism and Civilization: A History of Europe in our Time* (2009).[3] Neither of these works, both from British historians, possesses the range or depth of *Postwar*, but a new synthesis might soon be possible. Perhaps a successor to Judt, with a better distance from the events he describes, will craft a new narrative of Europe's recent past.

Future Directions

But one question stands in assessing Judt's successors: How difficult would it be to replace *Postwar*? It is enough to think of what it means to write a work of this kind. The author must be able to read in at least half a dozen major European languages, including a minimum of one Slavic language, to come to terms with Eastern European history. It would also be necessary to have a strong background in social, cultural, political, and economic history—along with the finances and time to travel extensively and work single-mindedly on the book for perhaps a decade.

Judt noted that he found all this necessary.[4] Who has the skills and resources to undertake a task of this magnitude? Timothy Snyder,* who worked with Judt on *Thinking the Twentieth Century*, is based at Yale University, an institution generous with time and money. He also has the language and historical skills to undertake a new postwar history. Most of his recent writing, however, has focused on World War II.[5]

In any case, many historians are now taking up the challenge of studying postwar Europe and combining Eastern and Western European history, as Judt did. A fine example of this kind of work is *Savage Continent: Europe in the Aftermath of World War II* (2012) by the writer and historian Keith Lowe.* In this work Lowe writes about Eastern and Western Europe in the postwar years.[6] Works on aspects of the history of this period exist, of course, but few can write, like Lowe and Judt, on both halves of postwar Europe. Lowe in fact notes in his introduction that *Postwar* stands as one of the very few books that achieves this.[7] Judt's legacy, then, may have been to create a new space—Eastern and Western Europe, 1945–2001—in which historians like Lowe can now carry out a broader, more ambitious kind of history.

Summary

Postwar ranks as one of the most remarkable works of history written in English in the last generation. Tony Judt managed, in 800-plus pages, to cover 50 years of a continent's past. This would represent a remarkable feat by any standards—but Judt refused to stick to simple political narrative, or ignore Europe's small- and medium-sized countries. In fact, he insisted on a wide definition of "Europe" to take in both the democratic West and the communist East. He bound these two disparate parts of the continent together in convincing fashion, citing their shared experience of World War II.

In *Postwar*, Judt also covered colorful subjects (such as the punk rock* explosion on the late 1970s), horrific subjects (war in the ex-Yugoslavia), and rather dry subjects (the management of nationalized companies in Spain under General Franco).*[8] Yet his prose style remains clear and often witty. For example, Judt describes the Croatian strong man Franjo Tudjman,* president between 1990 and his death in 1999, as being "notoriously ecumenical [roughly, all-inclusive] in his prejudices."[9] He wrote some parts of the book as conventional narrative, as when he described the collapse of the communist regimes.[10] Others were more analytical, such as Judt's magnificent epilogue on the Holocaust* in European memory.[11]

The result is a richly varied book that is still without rival as a description of Europe between World War II* (1945) and the collapse of the communist bloc (1989–91). Looking at the evolving societies and political systems of Eastern and Western Europe, Tony Judt saw a coherent whole that others before him had shied away from. In the process he brought a new understanding of how Europe changed, from the fall of Nazi Germany to the collapse of the Soviet bloc.

NOTES

1   Eric Hobsbawm, "After the Cold War," *London Review of Books* 34, no. 8 (April 26, 2012): 14; cf. Tony Judt with Timothy Snyder, *Thinking the Twentieth Century* (London: Penguin, 2012), 393.

2   See Tony Judt, *Postwar: A History of Europe since 1945* (New York: Penguin, 2005), 800.

3   Tom Buchanan, *Europe's Troubled Peace: 1945 to the Present* (London: Wiley-Blackwell, 2005); Bernard Wasserstein, *Barbarism and Civilization: A History of Europe in our Time* (Oxford: Oxford University Press, 2009).

4   Peter Jukes, "Tony Judt: The Last Interview," *Prospect*, August 2010, accessed October 20, 2015, http://www.prospectmagazine.co.uk/magazine/tony-judt-interview.

5   Timothy Snyder, *Bloodlands: Europe between Hitler and Stalin* (New York, Basic Books, 2010); Timothy Snyder, *Black Earth: The Holocaust as History and Warning* (New York: Tim Duggan Books, 2015).

6   Keith Lowe, *Savage Continent: Europe in the Aftermath of World War II* (London: Viking, 2012).

7   Lowe, *Savage Continent*, xvii.

8   Judt, *Postwar*, 481–2, 665–85, 556–67.

9   Judt, *Postwar*, 669.

10   Judt, *Postwar*, 585–664.

11   Judt, *Postwar*, 803–31.

GLOSSARY

GLOSSARY OF TERMS

Allies: the Western democratic powers (particularly Britain and the United States) and the Soviet Union. These fought Nazi Germany, Fascist Italy, and Imperial Japan in World War II.

Amyotrophic lateral sclerosis: a form of motor neuron disease that rapidly robs the body of all motor functions. It is also known as Lou Gehrig's disease, after the star New York Yankees baseball player who died from it.

***Annales* School:** a school of French historians active in France from the 1930s to the 1960s. *Annales* historians favored social history and particularly the study of long-term trends within society.

Anticolonialism: movements in Europe and in European colonies against colonialism—the policy of occupying and exploiting foreign territories and people.

Auschwitz: a Nazi extermination camp where prisoners (Jewish, gypsy, and other "enemy" groups) were worked, starved, and murdered with poison gas. It is estimated that as many as 1.5 million people died in this camp alone.

***Banlieues*:** a French word for "poor areas," often with high immigrant populations, on the outskirts of major French cities. The word has been increasingly used to describe poor areas in other parts of continental Europe as well.

The Beatles: a British pop band that became famous in 1962 and inspired many changes in international youth culture. The Beatles split up in 1970 after 12 albums.

Capitalism: an economic system based on private ownership and the free exchange of money and goods resulting in a free market.

Carnaby Street: a London street whose clothes shops were associated with the 1960s revolution in youth fashion.

Classical liberalism: a political creed that believes the state should intervene as little as possible in the market and life of the individual.

Cold War: a period between 1948 and 1991 when the United States and the Soviet Union were locked in a struggle for global political, cultural, and social influence. Given that both sides had, at least from the 1950s, significant nuclear arsenals, they chose to clash indirectly through proxy wars, espionage, and prestige contests.

Communism: a political system dedicated to state ownership of the economy and leading to the distribution of goods among citizens on a needs basis.

Cultural studies: a postwar academic discipline to study the shifting meanings and habits of contemporary culture. Cultural studies scholars tend to favor culture over economics as the key to modern societies.

Decolonization: the process by which the colonized nations in Asia, Africa, the Pacific, and the Americas claimed their independence from the European nations that had colonized them. Decolonization typically involved political and often violent protests.

Erich Maria Remarque Institute: an organization founded by Tony Judt in 1995 with financial backing from the widow of the German writer Erich Maria Remarque. The institute is primarily dedicated to the study of contemporary Europe.

Ethnic cleansing: the forced removal of ethnic groups from a given territory to provide areas with only one ethnic group.

Eugenics: a pseudoscience dedicated to improving human genetics through selective breeding and selective sterilization.

Euro debt crisis: a financial crisis, beginning in 2009, involving several European countries that could not pay their debts or debts incurred by local banks; all used the euro currency. The crisis has been dealt with through loans from other European Union countries and the International Monetary Fund.

European integration: a movement where, since 1949, a number of European powers have favored the idea of political and economic unity. This process, which is ongoing, would bring member states together in "ever closer union," according to the Treaty of Rome (1958).

European Union: a political and economic union formed in 1993 that consists of 28 member states.

Eurozone: term for the European Union countries that use the euro as their currency. Some European countries, including Poland and the United Kingdom, do not use the euro, either because they have opted out or because economic convergence has not yet been achieved.

Grammar schools: British state schools for students from 11 to 18 years of age, which operate on a selective principle. Children are only admitted after the successful completion of an exam at age 11.

Holocaust/Shoah: the murder of six million Jews and other persecuted minorities in World War II by the German Nazi regime. Many of those killed died in German extermination camps. It is also known as "the Shoah."

Hungarian Rising: an event that occurred in 1956, when the Hungarian government of Imre Nagy renounced communism and left the Warsaw Pact. The result was a Soviet invasion, which began on October 23, 1956 and quickly restored Soviet control of the country.

Marxism: the philosophy of Karl Marx (1818–83). Marx argued that history was driven by class struggle and that in his lifetime Britain and Germany had reached the age of capital. He advocated a revolution of working people to overthrow the capitalist system and install a society more attuned to individual worker needs.

Multiculturalism: the presence of different ethnic and religious groups, and an attempt on the part of the authorities to treat these different groups with equal respect.

Nationalism: a belief in the priority or even the supremacy of the nation in political matters, associated with chauvinism and sometimes racism.

Nazism: an extreme nationalist and racist form of authoritarian government built around the dictator Adolf Hitler; it was dominant in Germany from 1933 to 1945.

Neoliberalism: a contemporary version of nineteenth-century liberalism, particularly applied to a free-market economic model, often at the expense of national welfare systems.

Political history: the history of political ideas, political groups and institutions, and foreign relations; in the West, political history, particularly in narratives, has been the most popular form of history since ancient times.

Postwar consensus: the agreement in postwar Europe, involving parties on the left and right, to a series of social and economic questions that favored social democracy.

Pulitzer Prize: a series of 21 annual cultural prizes organized by Columbia University. These prizes include a nonfiction award, for which Tony Judt's *Postwar* was shortlisted.

Punk rock: a form of anarchic rock music that emerged in Britain in the late 1970s. Punk musicians were notorious for their willingness to shock.

Red Army Faction: an extreme leftist German terrorist group that carried out attacks on German soil and elsewhere in the 1970s.

Resistance: World War II partisan movements that fought the occupying Axis powers (Germany and Italy).

Russian Revolution: the 1917 event when the radical communist Bolsheviks took over the Russian state. Their revolution led to the creation of the Soviet Union.

Show trials: scripted court hearings held in the Soviet Union and, during the 1940s and 1950s, in its satellite states. These trials were often scripted and run to dispose publicly of "enemies of the people."

Social democracy: a social and economic system by which a state intervenes in a market economy to ameliorate poverty and to provide public services.

Socialism: a form of government in which the resources required for industrial production are held in public hands.

Sociology: the study of the functioning of human society and of social behavior.

Soviet Union: the name for communist Russia and the nearby states that the Russian communists had absorbed.

Structuralism: a system of thought that claims nothing in a society can be understood in isolation and that all components of a given society unite to create a structure that allows it to work.

Suez Crisis: an event in 1956 where Britain, France, and Israel agreed on a secret plan to seize control of the Suez Canal from the Egyptian government. The plan failed when the United States demanded that Britain and France end the operation. They did so: Britain reluctantly and France furiously.

"Total history": associated with the *Annales* School of historians, "total history" describes an approach in which the master themes of the history of a period are sought for both in institutional and political history and in the smallest specifics of social, religious, and cultural life.

Totalitarianism: a system of government that aspires to give all power to the state at the expense of the liberty of the individual citizen.

Welfare state: a system guaranteeing a minimum of economic assistance to vulnerable members of society, such as the unemployed, the elderly, and the ill.

World War I: a global conflict that lasted from 1914 to 1918, fought for the most part in Europe. The reparations demanded by the victorious powers (notably Britain, France, Russia, and the United States) of the losers (Germany and the Austro-Hungarian Empire), and the resentment they caused, are often considered a significant cause of World War II.

World War II: a global conflict that lasted from 1939 to 1945. It was fought, for the most part, in Europe, the Mediterranean, the northern Atlantic, and the Pacific between the Axis forces of Nazi Germany, Fascist Italy, and Imperial Japan, and the Allies, led by the Soviet Union, Great Britain, and the United States.

Zionism: a political and (increasingly) religious movement supporting the establishment of a Jewish homeland in Palestine, the site of ancient Israel.

PEOPLE MENTIONED IN THE TEXT

Bruce Bawer (b. 1956) is an American writer and poet, now a resident in Norway, who has written extensively on what he believes to be the increasing influence of Islam in Europe.

Tom Buchanan is a British professor of history at Oxford University, specializing in contemporary European history.

Norman Davies (b. 1939) is a British historian and specialist on Poland. Davies has written several notable popular histories including *Europe: A History* (1996).

Danny Dorling (b. 1968) is a British social geographer, based at Oxford University, who has written extensively on social inequality and social justice.

John Dunn (b. 1940) is a British political scientist who made his name by integrating historical analysis into his descriptions of Enlightenment thinkers.

General Franco (1892–1975) was the dictatorial right-wing leader of Spain between 1936 and his death. He took power following a nationalist revolution and victory in the civil war that followed.

François Furet (1927–97) was a French historian famous for his work on the French Revolution. Furet became disenchanted with communism and wrote *Passing of an Illusion* on this theme in 1995.

Johnny Hallyday (b. 1943) is a French pop singer and actor who became particularly popular in the 1960s.

Eric Hobsbawm (1917–2012) was a historian of German descent, born in Egypt, who moved to Britain, the country that became his home, in 1933. Hobsbawm was a Marxist who wrote on a wide range of modern and contemporary subjects.

Josef Joffe (b. 1944) is a German journalist and academic who has written extensively on the recent European past.

George Lichtheim (1912–73) was an anti-Soviet German Marxist historian who resettled in the United States and wrote a series of works on Western history and philosophy.

Keith Lowe (b. 1970) is a nonacademic British historian who has written on the events of World War II and its aftermath.

Jack Luzkow is a chair of the History, Philosophy and Religion Department and associate professor of history at Fontbonne University in St. Louis, Missouri.

Karl Marx (1818–83) was a highly influential economist and social theorist; Marxist theory, a method of social and historical analysis which emphasizes the struggle between the classes, among other things, is derived from his works, notably *Capital* (1867–94) and *The Communist Manifesto* (1848).

Mark Mazower (b. 1958) is a British historian who has written extensively on contemporary Europe. His best-known book is *Dark Continent* (1998), a history of twentieth-century Europe.

Alan Milward (1935–2010) was a British historian of European integration. Milward pointed to the often hidden economic and political motives behind early moves towards union in Europe.

Chris Patten (b. 1944) is a British conservative politician, last British governor of Hong Kong, and sometime author.

Kate Pickett (**b. 1965**) is professor of epidemiology at the University of York. She became famous in 2009 for publishing, with Richard Wilkinson, *The Spirit Level*. This work examined the negative effects of inequality in societies.

Jean-Paul Sartre (1905–80) was a French philosopher and a sometime fiction writer. He helped create existentialism and was loyal throughout most of his adult life to Soviet communism.

Quentin Skinner (b. 1940) is a British historian specializing in political thought. Skinner looked at the historical background of many Renaissance and early modern political thinkers.

Timothy Snyder (b. 1969) is an American historian based at Yale University, most famous for *Bloodlands* (2010), a description of the fate of Central Europe under Nazism and Stalinism.

Dan Stone is professor of contemporary history at the University of London.

A. J. P. Taylor (1906–90) was a British historian who wrote extensively on nineteenth- and twentieth-century European history. He is famous for popularizing contemporary history, particularly on British television.

Margaret Thatcher (1925–2013) was a British Conservative prime minister who served from 1979 to 1990. An economic liberal and hawkish in foreign affairs, she proved one of the most controversial British politicians of recent times.

Franjo Tudjman (1922–99) was president of Croatia from 1990 until his death in 1999. Tudjman has been accused of allowing and even supporting various atrocities against ethnically Serb populations within Croatia.

Bernard Wasserstein (b. 1948) is a British historian, specializing in twentieth-century history and particularly the Holocaust, currently based at the Ludwig Maximilians Universität, Munich.

Richard Wilkinson (b. 1943) is professor of social epidemiology at the University of Nottingham. He became famous in 2009 for publishing, with Kate Pickett, *The Spirit Level*. This work looked at the negative effects of inequality in societies.

WORKS CITED

WORKS CITED

Bawer, Bruce. "In the Shadow of the Gulag: Tony Judt's Europe." *The Hudson Review* 59, no. 4 (2007): 687–94.

Buchanan, Tom. *Europe's Troubled Peace: 1945 to the Present*. London: Wiley-Blackwell, 2005.

Burke, Peter. "The History of Events and the Revival of Narrative." In *New Perspectives on Historical Writing*, edited by Peter Burke, 233–48. University Park, PA: Penn State University Press, 1992.

Cesarani, David. "Introduction." In *After the Holocaust*, edited by David Cesarani and Eric Sundquist, 1–14. Abingdon: Routledge, 2012.

Dallas, Gregor. "Tony Judt: Historian of the Postwar Age." *GD-Frontiers*, 2005 [requested for *Literary Review* but then refused by the same]. Accessed November 1, 2015. http://www.gd-frontiers.net/spip.php?article11.

Davies, Norman. "The New European Century." *Guardian*, December 3, 2005. Accessed November 1, 2015. http://www.theguardian.com/books/2005/dec/03/featuresreviews.guardianreview4.

Davis, Donald E. and Eugene P. Trani. *The First Cold War: The Legacy of Woodrow Wilson in US–Soviet Relations*. Columbia, MO: University of Missouri Press, 2002.

Deák, István, Jan T. Gross, and Tony Judt, eds. *The Politics of Retribution in Europe: World War II and its Aftermath*. Princeton, NJ: Princeton University Press, 2000.

den Boer, Pim. "Historical Writing in France, 1800–1914." In *The Oxford History of Historical Writing: 1800–1945*, edited by Stuart Macintyre, Juan Maiguashca, and Attile Pók, 184–201. Oxford: Oxford University Press, 2011.

Dorling, Danny. *Injustice: Why Social Inequality Still Persists*. Bristol: Policy Press, 2015.

Dyrenfurth, Nick and Tim Soutphommasane, eds. *All That's Left: What Labor Should Stand For*. Sydney: University of New South Wales Press, 2010.

Dunn, John. *The Political Thought of John Locke*. Cambridge: Cambridge University Press, 1969.

Tony Judt's Twentieth Century. History Workshop Journal. Vol 75, no.1 (2013): 315.

Eley, Geoff. "Europe after 1945." *History Workshop Journal* 65 (2008): 195–212.

Feldman, David and John Lawrence. "Introduction: Structures and Transformations in British Historiography." In *Structures and Transformations in Modern British History*, edited by David Feldman and John Lawrence, 1–23. Cambridge: Cambridge University Press, 2011.

Freund, Michael. "A History of Two Europes" [interview with Judt]. *The Vienna Review*, October 1, 2006. Accessed October 20, 2015. http://www.viennareview. net/vienna-review-book-reviews/upcoming-literary-events/a-history-of-two-europes.

Furet, François. *The Passing of an Illusion: The Idea of Communism in the Twentieth Century*. Chicago, IL: University of Chicago Press, 1999.

Gaddis, John Lewis. *The Long Peace: Inquiries into the History of the Cold War*. Oxford: Oxford University Press, 1987.

Gillingham, John. *European Integration, 1950–2003: Superstate or New Market Economy?* Cambridge: Cambridge University Press, 2003.

Gray, John. "Postwar: A History of Europe since 1945, by Tony Judt." *The Independent*, October 28, 2005. Accessed February 25, 2016. http://www. independent.co.uk/arts-entertainment/books/reviews/postwar-a-history-of-europe-since-1945-by-tony-judt-322691.html

Hanhimäki, Jussi M. and Odd Arne Westad. *The Cold War: A History in Documents and Eyewitness Accounts*. Oxford: Oxford University Press, 2003.

Hayes, Peter. *How Was It Possible? A Holocaust Reader*. Lincoln, NE: University of Nebraska Press, 2015.

Hilson, Mary. *The Nordic Model: Scandinavia since 1945*. London: Reaktion, 2008.

Hobsbawm, Eric. "After the Cold War." *London Review of Books* 34, no. 8 (April 26, 2012): 14.

The Age of Capital, 1848–1875. London: Weidenfeld & Nicolson, 1975.

The Age of Empire, 1875–1914. London: Cardinal, 1987.

The Age of Extremes: The Short Twentieth Century, 1914–1991. London: Michael Joseph, 1994.

The Age of Revolution, 1789–1848. London: New English Library, 1965.

"Social History to the History of Society." Daedalus 100 (1971): 20–45.

Homans, Jennifer. "Introduction: In Good Faith." In Tony Judt, *When the Facts Change: Essays 1995–2010*, 1–10. London: William Heinemann, 2015.

Joffe, Josef. "The Worst of the West." *New York Times*, April 30, 2010. Accessed November 1, 2015. http://www.nytimes.com/2010/05/02/books/ review/Joffe-t.html?_r=0.

Johnson, Daniel. "Postwar by Tony Judt." *Commentary*, October 1, 2005. Accessed October 20, 2015. https://www.commentarymagazine.com/articles/postwar-by-tony-judt/.

Judt, Tony. *The Burden of Responsibility: Blum, Camus, Aron, and the French Twentieth Century*. Chicago, IL: University of Chicago Press, 1998.

"A Clown in Regal Purple: Social History and the Historians." *History Workshop Journal* 7 (1979): 66–94.

"Democracy as an Aberration." *New York Times*, February 7, 1999. Accessed October 24, 2015. https://www.nytimes.com/books/99/02/07/reviews/990207.07judtlt.html.

A Grand Illusion? An Essay on Europe. New York: Hill & Wang, 1996.

Ill Fares the Land. London: Allen Lane, 2010.

Marxism and the French Left: Studies on Labour and Politics in France, 1830–1981. Oxford: Oxford University Press, 1986.

The Memory Chalet. London: William Heinemann, 2010.

Past Imperfect: French Intellectuals, 1944–1956. Berkeley, CA: University of California Press, 1992.

Postwar: A History of Europe since 1945. New York: Penguin, 2005.

Postwar: A History of Europe since 1945, Audiobook. Ashland, OR: Blackstone Audio, 2011.

Reappraisals: Reflections on the Forgotten Twentieth Century. London: William Heinemann, 2008.

La reconstruction du Parti Socialiste, 1920–26. Paris: Fondation nationale des sciences politiques, 1976.

Socialism in Provence, 1871–1914: A Study in the Origins of the Modern French Left. Cambridge: Cambridge University Press, 1979.

When the Facts Change: Essays 1995–2010. London: William Heinemann, 2015.

Judt, Tony, ed. *Resistance and Revolution in Mediterranean Europe, 1939–1948*. London: Routledge, 1989.

Judt, Tony and Denis Lacorne, eds. *Language, Nation, and State: Identity Politics in a Multilingual Age*. Basingstoke: Palgrave Macmillan, 2004.

With Us or Against Us: Studies in Global Anti-Americanism. Basingstoke: Palgrave Macmillan, 2005.

Judt, Tony with Timothy Snyder. *Thinking the Twentieth Century*. London: Penguin, 2012.

Jukes, Peter. "Tony Judt: The Last Interview." *Prospect*, August 2010. Accessed October 20, 2015. http://www.prospectmagazine.co.uk/magazine/tony-judt-interview.

Klein, Menachem. *Lives in Common: Arabs and Jews in Jerusalem, Jaffa and Hebron*. London: Hurst & Co., 2014.

Kozlov, Denis. "Athens and Apocalypse: Writing History in the Soviet Union." In *Oxford History of Historical Writing: 1945 to the Present*, edited by Axel Schneider and Daniel Woolf, 375–98. Oxford: Oxford University Press, 2011.

Lichtheim, George. Europe in the Twentieth Century. London: Cardinal, 1974.

Lowe, Keith. *Savage Continent: Europe in the Aftermath of World War II*. London: Viking, 2012.

Luzkow, Jack. *The Great Forgetting: The Past, Present and Future of Social Democracy and the Welfare State.* Manchester: Manchester University Press, 2015.

Mazower, Mark. "Rebirth of a Continent." *New Statesman*, November 21, 2005. Accessed February 28, 2016. http://www.newstatesman.com/node/163306

Moyn, Samuel. "Intellectuals and Nazism." In *The Oxford Handbook of Postwar European History*, edited by Dan Stone, 671–91. Oxford: Oxford University Press, 2012.

Olesen, Thorsten Borring. "A Nordic Sonderweg to Europe: Integration History from a Northern Perspective." In *Northern Europe and the Future of the EU*, edited by Helge Hoibraaten and Jochen Hille, 35–48. Cambridge: Intersentia, 2011.

Painter, Anthony. *Left Without a Future: Social Justice in Anxious Times*. London: Taurus, 2013.

Patten, Chris. "Ill Fares the Land." *Guardian*, April 11, 2010. Accessed November 1, 2015. http://www.theguardian.com/books/2010/apr/11/ill-fares-land-tony-judt.

Patton, Stacey. "Wait, Your Footnotes Are in Cyberspace?" *Vitae*, August 18, 2014. Accessed October 20, 2015. https://chroniclevitae.com/news/665–wait-your-footnotes-are-in-cyberspace.

"Postwar Bibliography," accessed November 1, 2015, http://remarque.as.nyu.edu/docs/IO/9076/PostwarBibliography.pdf

Riley, Dylan. "Tony Judt: A Cooler Look." *New Left Review* 71 (2011): 31–63.

Skinner, Quentin. *Machiavelli*. Oxford: Oxford University Press, 1981.

Snyder, Timothy. *Black Earth: The Holocaust as History and Warning*. New York: Tim Duggan Books, 2015.

Bloodlands: Europe between Hitler and Stalin. New York: Basic Books, 2010.

Stone, Dan. "The Editor's Introduction." In *The Oxford Handbook of Postwar European History*, edited by Dan Stone, 1–33. Oxford: Oxford University Press, 2012.

Goodbye to All That? The Story of Europe since 1945. Oxford: Oxford University Press, 2014.

 Stone, Dan, ed. *The Oxford Handbook of Postwar European History*. Oxford: Oxford University Press, 2012.

Taulbee, James Larry, Ann Kelleher, and Peter C. Grosvenor. *Norway's Peace Policy: Soft Power in a Turbulent World*. New York: Palgrave Macmillan, 2014.

Taylor, A. J. P. *English History 1914–1945*. Oxford: Oxford University Press, 1965.

Wasserstein, Bernard. *Barbarism and Civilization: A History of Europe in our Time*. Oxford: Oxford University Press, 2009.

Wilkinson, Richard and Kate Pickett. *The Spirit Level: Why Greater Equality Makes Societies Stronger*. London: Bloomsbury Press, 2009.

THE MACAT LIBRARY
BY DISCIPLINE

AFRICANA STUDIES

Chinua Achebe's *An Image of Africa: Racism in Conrad's Heart of Darkness*
W. E. B. Du Bois's *The Souls of Black Folk*
Zora Neale Huston's *Characteristics of Negro Expression*
Martin Luther King Jr's *Why We Can't Wait*
Toni Morrison's *Playing in the Dark: Whiteness in the American Literary Imagination*

ANTHROPOLOGY

Arjun Appadurai's *Modernity at Large: Cultural Dimensions of Globalisation*
Philippe Ariès's *Centuries of Childhood*
Franz Boas's *Race, Language and Culture*
Kim Chan & Renée Mauborgne's *Blue Ocean Strategy*
Jared Diamond's *Guns, Germs & Steel: the Fate of Human Societies*
Jared Diamond's *Collapse: How Societies Choose to Fail or Survive*
E. E. Evans-Pritchard's *Witchcraft, Oracles and Magic Among the Azande*
James Ferguson's *The Anti-Politics Machine*
Clifford Geertz's *The Interpretation of Cultures*
David Graeber's *Debt: the First 5000 Years*
Karen Ho's *Liquidated: An Ethnography of Wall Street*
Geert Hofstede's *Culture's Consequences: Comparing Values, Behaviors, Institutes and Organizations across Nations*
Claude Lévi-Strauss's *Structural Anthropology*
Jay Macleod's *Ain't No Makin' It: Aspirations and Attainment in a Low-Income Neighborhood*
Saba Mahmood's *The Politics of Piety: The Islamic Revival and the Feminist Subject*
Marcel Mauss's *The Gift*

BUSINESS

Jean Lave & Etienne Wenger's *Situated Learning*
Theodore Levitt's *Marketing Myopia*
Burton G. Malkiel's *A Random Walk Down Wall Street*
Douglas McGregor's *The Human Side of Enterprise*
Michael Porter's *Competitive Strategy: Creating and Sustaining Superior Performance*
John Kotter's *Leading Change*
C. K. Prahalad & Gary Hamel's *The Core Competence of the Corporation*

CRIMINOLOGY

Michelle Alexander's *The New Jim Crow: Mass Incarceration in the Age of Colorblindness*
Michael R. Gottfredson & Travis Hirschi's *A General Theory of Crime*
Richard Herrnstein & Charles A. Murray's *The Bell Curve: Intelligence and Class Structure in American Life*
Elizabeth Loftus's *Eyewitness Testimony*
Jay Macleod's *Ain't No Makin' It: Aspirations and Attainment in a Low-Income Neighborhood*
Philip Zimbardo's *The Lucifer Effect*

ECONOMICS

Janet Abu-Lughod's *Before European Hegemony*
Ha-Joon Chang's *Kicking Away the Ladder*
David Brion Davis's *The Problem of Slavery in the Age of Revolution*
Milton Friedman's *The Role of Monetary Policy*
Milton Friedman's *Capitalism and Freedom*
David Graeber's *Debt: the First 5000 Years*
Friedrich Hayek's *The Road to Serfdom*
Karen Ho's *Liquidated: An Ethnography of Wall Street*

John Maynard Keynes's *The General Theory of Employment, Interest and Money*
Charles P. Kindleberger's *Manias, Panics and Crashes*
Robert Lucas's *Why Doesn't Capital Flow from Rich to Poor Countries?*
Burton G. Malkiel's *A Random Walk Down Wall Street*
Thomas Robert Malthus's *An Essay on the Principle of Population*
Karl Marx's *Capital*
Thomas Piketty's *Capital in the Twenty-First Century*
Amartya Sen's *Development as Freedom*
Adam Smith's *The Wealth of Nations*
Nassim Nicholas Taleb's *The Black Swan: The Impact of the Highly Improbable*
Amos Tversky's & Daniel Kahneman's *Judgment under Uncertainty: Heuristics and Biases*
Mahbub Ul Haq's *Reflections on Human Development*
Max Weber's *The Protestant Ethic and the Spirit of Capitalism*

FEMINISM AND GENDER STUDIES

Judith Butler's *Gender Trouble*
Simone De Beauvoir's *The Second Sex*
Michel Foucault's *History of Sexuality*
Betty Friedan's *The Feminine Mystique*
Saba Mahmood's *The Politics of Piety: The Islamic Revival and the Feminist Subjec*t
Joan Wallach Scott's *Gender and the Politics of History*
Mary Wollstonecraft's *A Vindication of the Rights of Woman*
Virginia Woolf's *A Room of One's Own*

GEOGRAPHY

The Brundtland Report's *Our Common Future*
Rachel Carson's *Silent Spring*
Charles Darwin's *On the Origin of Species*
James Ferguson's *The Anti-Politics Machine*
Jane Jacobs's *The Death and Life of Great American Cities*
James Lovelock's *Gaia: A New Look at Life on Earth*
Amartya Sen's *Development as Freedom*
Mathis Wackernagel & William Rees's *Our Ecological Footprint*

HISTORY

Janet Abu-Lughod's *Before European Hegemony*
Benedict Anderson's *Imagined Communities*
Bernard Bailyn's *The Ideological Origins of the American Revolution*
Hanna Batatu's *The Old Social Classes And The Revolutionary Movements Of Iraq*
Christopher Browning's *Ordinary Men: Reserve Police Batallion 101 and the Final Solution in Poland*
Edmund Burke's *Reflections on the Revolution in France*
William Cronon's *Nature's Metropolis: Chicago And The Great West*
Alfred W. Crosby's *The Columbian Exchange*
Hamid Dabashi's *Iran: A People Interrupted*
David Brion Davis's *The Problem of Slavery in the Age of Revolution*
Nathalie Zemon Davis's *The Return of Martin Guerre*
Jared Diamond's *Guns, Germs & Steel: the Fate of Human Societies*
Frank Dikotter's *Mao's Great Famine*
John W Dower's *War Without Mercy: Race And Power In The Pacific War*
W. E. B. Du Bois's *The Souls of Black Folk*
Richard J. Evans's *In Defence of History*
Lucien Febvre's *The Problem of Unbelief in the 16th Century*
Sheila Fitzpatrick's *Everyday Stalinism*

The Macat Library By Discipline

Eric Foner's *Reconstruction: America's Unfinished Revolution, 1863-1877*
Michel Foucault's *Discipline and Punish*
Michel Foucault's *History of Sexuality*
Francis Fukuyama's *The End of History and the Last Man*
John Lewis Gaddis's *We Now Know: Rethinking Cold War History*
Ernest Gellner's *Nations and Nationalism*
Eugene Genovese's *Roll, Jordan, Roll: The World the Slaves Made*
Carlo Ginzburg's *The Night Battles*
Daniel Goldhagen's *Hitler's Willing Executioners*
Jack Goldstone's *Revolution and Rebellion in the Early Modern World*
Antonio Gramsci's *The Prison Notebooks*
Alexander Hamilton, John Jay & James Madison's *The Federalist Papers*
Christopher Hill's *The World Turned Upside Down*
Carole Hillenbrand's *The Crusades: Islamic Perspectives*
Thomas Hobbes's *Leviathan*
Eric Hobsbawm's *The Age Of Revolution*
John A. Hobson's *Imperialism: A Study*
Albert Hourani's *History of the Arab Peoples*
Samuel P. Huntington's *The Clash of Civilizations and the Remaking of World Order*
C. L. R. James's *The Black Jacobins*
Tony Judt's *Postwar: A History of Europe Since 1945*
Ernst Kantorowicz's *The King's Two Bodies: A Study in Medieval Political Theology*
Paul Kennedy's *The Rise and Fall of the Great Powers*
Ian Kershaw's *The "Hitler Myth": Image and Reality in the Third Reich*
John Maynard Keynes's *The General Theory of Employment, Interest and Money*
Charles P. Kindleberger's *Manias, Panics and Crashes*
Martin Luther King Jr's *Why We Can't Wait*
Henry Kissinger's *World Order: Reflections on the Character of Nations and the Course of History*
Thomas Kuhn's *The Structure of Scientific Revolutions*
Georges Lefebvre's *The Coming of the French Revolution*
John Locke's *Two Treatises of Government*
Niccolò Machiavelli's *The Prince*
Thomas Robert Malthus's *An Essay on the Principle of Population*
Mahmood Mamdani's *Citizen and Subject: Contemporary Africa And The Legacy Of Late Colonialism*
Karl Marx's *Capital*
Stanley Milgram's *Obedience to Authority*
John Stuart Mill's *On Liberty*
Thomas Paine's *Common Sense*
Thomas Paine's *Rights of Man*
Geoffrey Parker's *Global Crisis: War, Climate Change and Catastrophe in the Seventeenth Century*
Jonathan Riley-Smith's *The First Crusade and the Idea of Crusading*
Jean-Jacques Rousseau's *The Social Contract*
Joan Wallach Scott's *Gender and the Politics of History*
Theda Skocpol's *States and Social Revolutions*
Adam Smith's *The Wealth of Nations*
Timothy Snyder's *Bloodlands: Europe Between Hitler and Stalin*
Sun Tzu's *The Art of War*
Keith Thomas's *Religion and the Decline of Magic*
Thucydides's *The History of the Peloponnesian War*
Frederick Jackson Turner's *The Significance of the Frontier in American History*
Odd Arne Westad's *The Global Cold War: Third World Interventions And The Making Of Our Times*

The Macat Library By Discipline

LITERATURE

Chinua Achebe's *An Image of Africa: Racism in Conrad's Heart of Darkness*
Roland Barthes's *Mythologies*
Homi K. Bhabha's *The Location of Culture*
Judith Butler's *Gender Trouble*
Simone De Beauvoir's *The Second Sex*
Ferdinand De Saussure's *Course in General Linguistics*
T. S. Eliot's *The Sacred Wood: Essays on Poetry and Criticism*
Zora Neale Huston's *Characteristics of Negro Expression*
Toni Morrison's *Playing in the Dark: Whiteness in the American Literary Imagination*
Edward Said's *Orientalism*
Gayatri Chakravorty Spivak's *Can the Subaltern Speak?*
Mary Wollstonecraft's *A Vindication of the Rights of Women*
Virginia Woolf's *A Room of One's Own*

PHILOSOPHY

Elizabeth Anscombe's *Modern Moral Philosophy*
Hannah Arendt's *The Human Condition*
Aristotle's *Metaphysics*
Aristotle's *Nicomachean Ethics*
Edmund Gettier's *Is Justified True Belief Knowledge?*
Georg Wilhelm Friedrich Hegel's *Phenomenology of Spirit*
David Hume's *Dialogues Concerning Natural Religion*
David Hume's *The Enquiry for Human Understanding*
Immanuel Kant's *Religion within the Boundaries of Mere Reason*
Immanuel Kant's *Critique of Pure Reason*
Søren Kierkegaard's *The Sickness Unto Death*
Søren Kierkegaard's *Fear and Trembling*
C. S. Lewis's *The Abolition of Man*
Alasdair MacIntyre's *After Virtue*
Marcus Aurelius's *Meditations*
Friedrich Nietzsche's *On the Genealogy of Morality*
Friedrich Nietzsche's *Beyond Good and Evil*
Plato's *Republic*
Plato's *Symposium*
Jean-Jacques Rousseau's *The Social Contract*
Gilbert Ryle's *The Concept of Mind*
Baruch Spinoza's *Ethics*
Sun Tzu's *The Art of War*
Ludwig Wittgenstein's *Philosophical Investigations*

POLITICS

Benedict Anderson's *Imagined Communities*
Aristotle's *Politics*
Bernard Bailyn's *The Ideological Origins of the American Revolution*
Edmund Burke's *Reflections on the Revolution in France*
John C. Calhoun's *A Disquisition on Government*
Ha-Joon Chang's *Kicking Away the Ladder*
Hamid Dabashi's *Iran: A People Interrupted*
Hamid Dabashi's *Theology of Discontent: The Ideological Foundation of the Islamic Revolution in Iran*
Robert Dahl's *Democracy and its Critics*
Robert Dahl's *Who Governs?*
David Brion Davis's *The Problem of Slavery in the Age of Revolution*

The Macat Library By Discipline

Alexis De Tocqueville's *Democracy in America*
James Ferguson's *The Anti-Politics Machine*
Frank Dikotter's *Mao's Great Famine*
Sheila Fitzpatrick's *Everyday Stalinism*
Eric Foner's *Reconstruction: America's Unfinished Revolution, 1863-1877*
Milton Friedman's *Capitalism and Freedom*
Francis Fukuyama's *The End of History and the Last Man*
John Lewis Gaddis's *We Now Know: Rethinking Cold War History*
Ernest Gellner's *Nations and Nationalism*
David Graeber's *Debt: the First 5000 Years*
Antonio Gramsci's *The Prison Notebooks*
Alexander Hamilton, John Jay & James Madison's *The Federalist Papers*
Friedrich Hayek's *The Road to Serfdom*
Christopher Hill's *The World Turned Upside Down*
Thomas Hobbes's *Leviathan*
John A. Hobson's *Imperialism: A Study*
Samuel P. Huntington's *The Clash of Civilizations and the Remaking of World Order*
Tony Judt's *Postwar: A History of Europe Since 1945*
David C. Kang's *China Rising: Peace, Power and Order in East Asia*
Paul Kennedy's *The Rise and Fall of Great Powers*
Robert Keohane's *After Hegemony*
Martin Luther King Jr.'s *Why We Can't Wait*
Henry Kissinger's *World Order: Reflections on the Character of Nations and the Course of History*
John Locke's *Two Treatises of Government*
Niccolò Machiavelli's *The Prince*
Thomas Robert Malthus's *An Essay on the Principle of Population*
Mahmood Mamdani's *Citizen and Subject: Contemporary Africa And The Legacy Of Late Colonialism*
Karl Marx's *Capital*
John Stuart Mill's *On Liberty*
John Stuart Mill's *Utilitarianism*
Hans Morgenthau's *Politics Among Nations*
Thomas Paine's *Common Sense*
Thomas Paine's *Rights of Man*
Thomas Piketty's *Capital in the Twenty-First Century*
Robert D. Putman's *Bowling Alone*
John Rawls's *Theory of Justice*
Jean-Jacques Rousseau's *The Social Contract*
Theda Skocpol's *States and Social Revolutions*
Adam Smith's *The Wealth of Nations*
Sun Tzu's *The Art of War*
Henry David Thoreau's *Civil Disobedience*
Thucydides's *The History of the Peloponnesian War*
Kenneth Waltz's *Theory of International Politics*
Max Weber's *Politics as a Vocation*
Odd Arne Westad's *The Global Cold War: Third World Interventions And The Making Of Our Times*

POSTCOLONIAL STUDIES

Roland Barthes's *Mythologies*
Frantz Fanon's *Black Skin, White Masks*
Homi K. Bhabha's *The Location of Culture*
Gustavo Gutiérrez's *A Theology of Liberation*
Edward Said's *Orientalism*
Gayatri Chakravorty Spivak's *Can the Subaltern Speak?*

PSYCHOLOGY

Gordon Allport's *The Nature of Prejudice*
Alan Baddeley & Graham Hitch's *Aggression: A Social Learning Analysis*
Albert Bandura's *Aggression: A Social Learning Analysis*
Leon Festinger's *A Theory of Cognitive Dissonance*
Sigmund Freud's *The Interpretation of Dreams*
Betty Friedan's *The Feminine Mystique*
Michael R. Gottfredson & Travis Hirschi's *A General Theory of Crime*
Eric Hoffer's *The True Believer: Thoughts on the Nature of Mass Movements*
William James's *Principles of Psychology*
Elizabeth Loftus's *Eyewitness Testimony*
A. H. Maslow's *A Theory of Human Motivation*
Stanley Milgram's *Obedience to Authority*
Steven Pinker's *The Better Angels of Our Nature*
Oliver Sacks's *The Man Who Mistook His Wife For a Hat*
Richard Thaler & Cass Sunstein's *Nudge: Improving Decisions About Health, Wealth and Happiness*
Amos Tversky's *Judgment under Uncertainty: Heuristics and Biases*
Philip Zimbardo's *The Lucifer Effect*

SCIENCE

Rachel Carson's *Silent Spring*
William Cronon's *Nature's Metropolis: Chicago And The Great West*
Alfred W. Crosby's *The Columbian Exchange*
Charles Darwin's *On the Origin of Species*
Richard Dawkin's *The Selfish Gene*
Thomas Kuhn's *The Structure of Scientific Revolutions*
Geoffrey Parker's *Global Crisis: War, Climate Change and Catastrophe in the Seventeenth Century*
Mathis Wackernagel & William Rees's *Our Ecological Footprint*

SOCIOLOGY

Michelle Alexander's *The New Jim Crow: Mass Incarceration in the Age of Colorblindness*
Gordon Allport's *The Nature of Prejudice*
Albert Bandura's *Aggression: A Social Learning Analysis*
Hanna Batatu's *The Old Social Classes And The Revolutionary Movements Of Iraq*
Ha-Joon Chang's *Kicking Away the Ladder*
W. E. B. Du Bois's *The Souls of Black Folk*
Émile Durkheim's *On Suicide*
Frantz Fanon's *Black Skin, White Masks*
Frantz Fanon's *The Wretched of the Earth*
Eric Foner's *Reconstruction: America's Unfinished Revolution, 1863-1877*
Eugene Genovese's *Roll, Jordan, Roll: The World the Slaves Made*
Jack Goldstone's *Revolution and Rebellion in the Early Modern World*
Antonio Gramsci's *The Prison Notebooks*
Richard Herrnstein & Charles A Murray's *The Bell Curve: Intelligence and Class Structure in American Life*
Eric Hoffer's *The True Believer: Thoughts on the Nature of Mass Movements*
Jane Jacobs's *The Death and Life of Great American Cities*
Robert Lucas's *Why Doesn't Capital Flow from Rich to Poor Countries?*
Jay Macleod's *Ain't No Makin' It: Aspirations and Attainment in a Low Income Neighborhood*
Elaine May's *Homeward Bound: American Families in the Cold War Era*
Douglas McGregor's *The Human Side of Enterprise*
C. Wright Mills's *The Sociological Imagination*

Thomas Piketty's *Capital in the Twenty-First Century*
Robert D. Putman's *Bowling Alone*
David Riesman's *The Lonely Crowd: A Study of the Changing American Character*
Edward Said's *Orientalism*
Joan Wallach Scott's *Gender and the Politics of History*
Theda Skocpol's *States and Social Revolutions*
Max Weber's *The Protestant Ethic and the Spirit of Capitalism*

THEOLOGY

Augustine's *Confessions*
Benedict's *Rule of St Benedict*
Gustavo Gutiérrez's *A Theology of Liberation*
Carole Hillenbrand's *The Crusades: Islamic Perspectives*
David Hume's *Dialogues Concerning Natural Religion*
Immanuel Kant's *Religion within the Boundaries of Mere Reason*
Ernst Kantorowicz's *The King's Two Bodies: A Study in Medieval Political Theology*
Søren Kierkegaard's *The Sickness Unto Death*
C. S. Lewis's *The Abolition of Man*
Saba Mahmood's *The Politics of Piety: The Islamic Revival and the Feminist Subject*
Baruch Spinoza's *Ethics*
Keith Thomas's *Religion and the Decline of Magic*

COMING SOON

Chris Argyris's *The Individual and the Organisation*
Seyla Benhabib's *The Rights of Others*
Walter Benjamin's *The Work Of Art in the Age of Mechanical Reproduction*
John Berger's *Ways of Seeing*
Pierre Bourdieu's *Outline of a Theory of Practice*
Mary Douglas's *Purity and Danger*
Roland Dworkin's *Taking Rights Seriously*
James G. March's *Exploration and Exploitation in Organisational Learning*
Ikujiro Nonaka's *A Dynamic Theory of Organizational Knowledge Creation*
Griselda Pollock's *Vision and Difference*
Amartya Sen's *Inequality Re-Examined*
Susan Sontag's *On Photography*
Yasser Tabbaa's *The Transformation of Islamic Art*
Ludwig von Mises's *Theory of Money and Credit*

Macat Disciplines

Access the greatest ideas and thinkers across entire disciplines, including

AFRICANA STUDIES

Chinua Achebe's *An Image of Africa: Racism in Conrad's Heart of Darkness*

W. E. B. Du Bois's *The Souls of Black Folk*

Zora Neale Hurston's *Characteristics of Negro Expression*

Martin Luther King Jr.'s *Why We Can't Wait*

Toni Morrison's *Playing in the Dark: Whiteness in the American Literary Imagination*

Macat analyses are available from all good bookshops and libraries.

Access hundreds of analyses through one, multimedia tool.
Join free for one month **library.macat.com**

Macat Disciplines

Access the greatest ideas and thinkers across entire disciplines, including

FEMINISM, GENDER AND QUEER STUDIES

Simone De Beauvoir's
The Second Sex

Michel Foucault's
History of Sexuality

Betty Friedan's
The Feminine Mystique

Saba Mahmood's
*The Politics of Piety:
The Islamic Revival and
the Feminist Subject*

Joan Wallach Scott's
*Gender and the
Politics of History*

Mary Wollstonecraft's
*A Vindication of the
Rights of Woman*

Virginia Woolf's
A Room of One's Own

Judith Butler's
Gender Trouble

 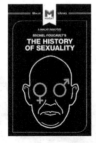  

Macat Disciplines

*Access the greatest ideas and thinkers
across entire disciplines, including*

CRIMINOLOGY

Michelle Alexander's
*The New Jim Crow:
Mass Incarceration in the
Age of Colorblindness*

**Michael R. Gottfredson
& Travis Hirschi's**
A General Theory of Crime

Elizabeth Loftus's
Eyewitness Testimony

**Richard Herrnstein
& Charles A. Murray's**
*The Bell Curve: Intelligence and
Class Structure in American Life*

Jay Macleod's
*Ain't No Makin' It:
Aspirations and Attainment in a
Low-Income Neighborhood*

Philip Zimbardo's
The Lucifer Effect

Macat analyses are available from all good bookshops and libraries.

Access hundreds of analyses through one, multimedia tool.
Join free for one month **library.macat.com**

Macat Disciplines

Access the greatest ideas and thinkers across entire disciplines, including

INEQUALITY

Ha-Joon Chang's, *Kicking Away the Ladder*

David Graeber's, *Debt: The First 5000 Years*

Robert E. Lucas's, *Why Doesn't Capital Flow from Rich To Poor Countries?*

Thomas Piketty's, *Capital in the Twenty-First Century*

Amartya Sen's, *Inequality Re-Examined*

Mahbub Ul Haq's, *Reflections on Human Development*

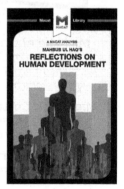

Macat Disciplines

Access the greatest ideas and thinkers across entire disciplines, including

GLOBALIZATION

Arjun Appadurai's, *Modernity at Large: Cultural Dimensions of Globalisation*

James Ferguson's, *The Anti-Politics Machine*

Geert Hofstede's, *Culture's Consequences*

Amartya Sen's, *Development as Freedom*

Macat analyses are available from all good bookshops and libraries.

Access hundreds of analyses through one, multimedia tool.
Join free for one month **library.macat.com**

Macat Disciplines

Access the greatest ideas and thinkers across entire disciplines, including

THE FUTURE OF DEMOCRACY

Robert A. Dahl's, *Democracy and Its Critics*
Robert A. Dahl's, *Who Governs?*
Alexis De Toqueville's, *Democracy in America*
Niccolò Machiavelli's, *The Prince*
John Stuart Mill's, *On Liberty*
Robert D. Putnam's, *Bowling Alone*
Jean-Jacques Rousseau's, *The Social Contract*
Henry David Thoreau's, *Civil Disobedience*

Macat Disciplines

Access the greatest ideas and thinkers across entire disciplines, including

TOTALITARIANISM

Sheila Fitzpatrick's, *Everyday Stalinism*
Ian Kershaw's, *The "Hitler Myth"*
Timothy Snyder's, *Bloodlands*

Macat Pairs

Analyse historical and modern issues from opposite sides of an argument. Pairs include:

RACE AND IDENTITY

Zora Neale Hurston's
Characteristics of Negro Expression

Using material collected on anthropological expeditions to the South, Zora Neale Hurston explains how expression in African American culture in the early twentieth century departs from the art of white America. At the time, African American art was often criticized for copying white culture. For Hurston, this criticism misunderstood how art works. European tradition views art as something fixed. But Hurston describes a creative process that is alive, ever-changing, and largely improvisational. She maintains that African American art works through a process called 'mimicry'—where an imitated object or verbal pattern, for example, is reshaped and altered until it becomes something new, novel—and worthy of attention.

Frantz Fanon's
Black Skin, White Masks

Black Skin, White Masks offers a radical analysis of the psychological effects of colonization on the colonized.

Fanon witnessed the effects of colonization first hand both in his birthplace, Martinique, and again later in life when he worked as a psychiatrist in another French colony, Algeria. His text is uncompromising in form and argument. He dissects the dehumanizing effects of colonialism, arguing that it destroys the native sense of identity, forcing people to adapt to an alien set of values—including a core belief that they are inferior. This results in deep psychological trauma.

Fanon's work played a pivotal role in the civil rights movements of the 1960s.

Macat analyses are available from all good bookshops and libraries.

Access hundreds of analyses through one, multimedia tool.
Join free for one month **library.macat.com**

Macat Pairs

Analyse historical and modern issues from opposite sides of an argument. Pairs include:

INTERNATIONAL RELATIONS IN THE 21ST CENTURY

Samuel P. Huntington's
The Clash of Civilisations

In his highly influential 1996 book, Huntington offers a vision of a post-Cold War world in which conflict takes place not between competing ideologies but between cultures. The worst clash, he argues, will be between the Islamic world and the West: the West's arrogance and belief that its culture is a "gift" to the world will come into conflict with Islam's obstinacy and concern that its culture is under attack from a morally decadent "other."

Clash inspired much debate between different political schools of thought. But its greatest impact came in helping define American foreign policy in the wake of the 2001 terrorist attacks in New York and Washington.

Francis Fukuyama's
The End of History and the Last Man

Published in 1992, *The End of History and the Last Man* argues that capitalist democracy is the final destination for all societies. Fukuyama believed democracy triumphed during the Cold War because it lacks the "fundamental contradictions" inherent in communism and satisfies our yearning for freedom and equality. Democracy therefore marks the endpoint in the evolution of ideology, and so the "end of history." There will still be "events," but no fundamental change in ideology.

Macat Pairs

Analyse historical and modern issues from opposite sides of an argument. Pairs include:

MACAT

MACAT

HOW TO RUN AN ECONOMY

John Maynard Keynes's
The General Theory OF Employment, Interest and Money

Classical economics suggests that market economies are self-correcting in times of recession or depression, and tend toward full employment and output. But English economist John Maynard Keynes disagrees.

In his ground-breaking 1936 study *The General Theory*, Keynes argues that traditional economics has misunderstood the causes of unemployment. Employment is not determined by the price of labor; it is directly linked to demand. Keynes believes market economies are by nature unstable, and so require government intervention. Spurred on by the social catastrophe of the Great Depression of the 1930s, he sets out to revolutionize the way the world thinks

Milton Friedman's
The Role of Monetary Policy

Friedman's 1968 paper changed the course of economic theory. In just 17 pages, he demolished existing theory and outlined an effective alternate monetary policy designed to secure 'high employment, stable prices and rapid growth.'

Friedman demonstrated that monetary policy plays a vital role in broader economic stability and argued that economists got their monetary policy wrong in the 1950s and 1960s by misunderstanding the relationship between inflation and unemployment. Previous generations of economists had believed that governments could permanently decrease unemployment by permitting inflation—and vice versa. Friedman's most original contribution was to show that this supposed trade-off is an illusion that only works in the short term.

Macat analyses are available from all good bookshops and libraries.

Access hundreds of analyses through one, multimedia tool.
Join free for one month **library.macat.com**

Macat Pairs

Analyse historical and modern issues from opposite sides of an argument. Pairs include:

ARE WE FUNDAMENTALLY GOOD - OR BAD?

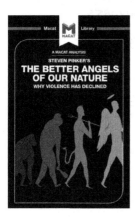

Steven Pinker's
The Better Angels of Our Nature

Stephen Pinker's gloriously optimistic 2011 book argues that, despite humanity's biological tendency toward violence, we are, in fact, less violent today than ever before. To prove his case, Pinker lays out pages of detailed statistical evidence. For him, much of the credit for the decline goes to the eighteenth-century Enlightenment movement, whose ideas of liberty, tolerance, and respect for the value of human life filtered down through society and affected how people thought. That psychological change led to behavioral change—and overall we became more peaceful. Critics countered that humanity could never overcome the biological urge toward violence; others argued that Pinker's statistics were flawed.

Philip Zimbardo's
The Lucifer Effect

Some psychologists believe those who commit cruelty are innately evil. Zimbardo disagrees. In *The Lucifer Effect*, he argues that sometimes good people do evil things simply because of the situations they find themselves in, citing many historical examples to illustrate his point. Zimbardo details his 1971 Stanford prison experiment, where ordinary volunteers playing guards in a mock prison rapidly became abusive. But he also describes the tortures committed by US army personnel in Iraq's Abu Ghraib prison in 2003—and how he himself testified in defence of one of those guards. committed by US army personnel in Iraq's Abu Ghraib prison in 2003—and how he himself testified in defence of one of those guards.

Macat analyses are available from all good bookshops and libraries.

Access hundreds of analyses through one, multimedia tool.
Join free for one month **library.macat.com**

Macat Pairs

Analyse historical and modern issues from opposite sides of an argument. Pairs include:

HOW WE RELATE TO EACH OTHER AND SOCIETY

Jean-Jacques Rousseau's
The Social Contract

Rousseau's famous work sets out the radical concept of the 'social contract': a give-and-take relationship between individual freedom and social order.

If people are free to do as they like, governed only by their own sense of justice, they are also vulnerable to chaos and violence. To avoid this, Rousseau proposes, they should agree to give up some freedom to benefit from the protection of social and political organization. But this deal is only just if societies are led by the collective needs and desires of the people, and able to control the private interests of individuals. For Rousseau, the only legitimate form of government is rule by the people.

Robert D. Putnam's
Bowling Alone

In *Bowling Alone*, Robert Putnam argues that Americans have become disconnected from one another and from the institutions of their common life, and investigates the consequences of this change.

Looking at a range of indicators, from membership in formal organizations to the number of invitations being extended to informal dinner parties, Putnam demonstrates that Americans are interacting less and creating less "social capital" – with potentially disastrous implications for their society.

It would be difficult to overstate the impact of *Bowling Alone*, one of the most frequently cited social science publications of the last half-century.

Printed in the United States
by Baker & Taylor Publisher Services